MIND
MATTERS

by

Marguerite Iwersen

DeVorss & Co., Publishers
P.O. Box 550
Marina del Rey, CA 90291

ISBN: 0-87516-421-8

Library of Congress Card Catalog Number:
80-67158

Printed in the United States of America
by Book Graphics, Inc., Marina del Rey, California

To those who, through the years, have shared many of
these thoughts in our search for a
Way for Today

CONTENTS

vii

ACKNOWLEDGMENTS

Grateful acknowledgment is made to the
following authors and publishers for
permission to quote copyrighted
material from their books

ALVIN TOFFLER, *Future Shock* (Copyright 1970 by Alvin Toffler, published by Random House, Inc., N.Y.)

FRANK G. GOBLE, *The Third Force,* with introduction by Abraham Maslow (Copyright 1970 by Thomas Jefferson Research Center, excerpts from introduction reprinted by permission of Grossman Publishers, a Division of Viking Penguin, Inc.)

LECOMTE DU NOÜY, *Human Destiny* (Copyright 1947 by Lecomte du Noüy, published by Longman's Green & Co., Inc., permission granted by David McKay Company, Inc.)

ABRAHAM H. MASLOW, *Religions, Values and Peak Experiences* (Copyright 1964 by Viking Press, used by permission of Kappa Delta Pi, P. O. Box A, West Lafayette, Indiana, 47906.)

LINCOLN BARNETT, *The Universe and Dr. Einstein* (Copyright 1957 by Lincoln Barnett, Publishers Harper & Brothers, now controlled by William Morrow & Company, Inc.)

H.G. WELLS, *Outline of History* (Copyright 1921 by Doubleday & Company, permission granted by A. P. Watts, Ltd., London.)

PART ONE

Chapter One

MAN UPROOTED

Sally unlocked her apartment door, entered and kicked it shut. Three times she kicked it, saying "Phui" each time. She threw her mink coat into the nearest chair and sat herself on top. Then she threw her purse and gloves across the room, "Bah." Soon she strode to the bar, "No ice, dammit." With her lukewarm Scotch she stalked across the room, gulping down big mouthfuls and choking a little on each gulp. At refill time she blurted out, "Home, phui! Sham! Showplace!" After the third refill she picked up a pillow from the couch, flung it to the floor and stamped on it. "No more couches, no more messing around, phui! Nothing is real—nothing." With the next drink she stumbled against the couch, swore, and slumped down on it. The full glass spilled onto the rug. "Goddammit," she muttered. After a while there was a helpless little wail—"Wish I believed in God."

A few city blocks away in an apartment kitchen Tom was putting one lone frozen dinner into the oven. Daughter Jane, sixteen, pregnant, had left a note saying she would be out. "Probably that kooky gang . . . just hope it's not cocaine," he thought. "Wish she'd open up to me. Nothing I can do, just wait. At least she did leave a note." During the World News Tom's feelings nagged at him. "Mars, Venus, Jupiter, who cares? What good to me are

3

samples of moon dust? I don't belong on the moon, I
don't even belong here, or anywhere, to anybody." When
the timer sounded he put the drippy hot dinner on a tray,
sat near the television set and forked up the food. Now
and then he glanced at "Last of the Wild." "Yes, endangered; so are we, Sally, Jane and I. But who cares?"

His own word "endangered" startled him so that he left
the smelly cigarette stub in the ashtray and quickly went
through the motions of clearing the kitchen. "Example
for Jane," he mumbled as he snapped off the light. The
routine: Time Magazine, pay bills, late news, bed. He
flopped over several times, found himself sitting bolt up-
right punching the pillow; tired of listening for Jane, he
dropped into sleep.

The word "endangered" is sometimes shrugged off as
applying to such creatures as parrots, crocodiles and seals;
but—anxious father, hanging on to his humdrum position
so as to pay alimony to luxury loving wife—Tom could
not shrug it off. He had not deliberately said the word, it
just slipped out; suddenly he knew it was the truth, not
only for his own uprooted family but for millions and millions in the Christian world. It actually *is* the truth. Ecolo-
gists, more and more vociferous about man's ruining the
earth's crust, make plans to farm the ocean floor and col-
onize space. But far more than the environment is endangered; humanity's mind, heart and soul have for decades
been in decline. Since the mid-sixties two distinguished
humanists, Lewis Mumford and Alvin Toffler, for instance, have been warning of impending cataclysm.

On the jacket of Toffler's book *Future Shock* is the
blurb—"This book can help us survive our collision with
tomorrow." Within its pages a quotation reads: "Not
even the most brilliant scientist knows where science is taking us. We are aboard a train which is gathering speed,

racing down a track where there are an unknown number of switches leading to unknown destinations. No single scientist is in the engine cab, and there may be demons at the switch. Most of society is in the caboose, looking backward.''

Sally and her jet set do not bother with such warnings. Only the immediate extravagances, excitements and orgies matter. Psychotherapy left Sally's ego problems unsolved. As if on a treadmill she still repeats, "freedom . . . fun . . . not Tom . . . not Dad . . . Where's Mother? She'd care! Look at Jane, three more months, then what? . . . She hates me . . . Oh God!'' Meantime Sally has her maid, her car, her beauty treatments. She does all the smart things like a mechanical doll that runs on alcohol.

Life in the 'developed West' is largely mechanical. Tom goes through the mechanics of analyzing. Media machines, space machines, war machines, hospital machines, college machines, government machines, tax machines, all chug away endlessly. Everyone is geared to the machine he operates. Huge institutions suction in hordes of people by day and spew them forth at night. Restaurant machines, cinema or disco machines then take over. Hundreds of thousands bounce into unemployment, then into welfare machines. Humans today are as empty and helpless as ping-pong balls being whanged about. More and more 'doing' and less and less 'be-ing.' To be tolerated one puts on a front and goes through the motions of being efficient, well adjusted—even jovial. Otherwise—psychotherapy, crime and then drugs.

Tom, Jane and Sally are moderates, still going through the motions. They represent the kind of client described by psychiatrist Rollo May in his *Man's Search For Himself*. Writing in the early fifties he spoke of the hollow people, anxious and powerless. Far from having specific personal

problems to be analyzed away, they were so de-personal-
ized, so 'conforming' that they could not define any private goals. While trying to play it cool, to be intellectual or
scientific or sophisticated, they became empty of feeling,
empty of any real identity. By the late sixties Rollo May
found that these already hollow people were sliding deeper
into lethargy, lostness, even desperation. They had become care-less, without love, hope-less and without will.
Nothing issued forth from within them; all excitement and
activity had to come from the outer world.

Now, in the late seventies, it seems, those in the English
speaking world who read books have become vaguely
aware of their inner emptiness. According to the best seller
lists, they buy untold millions of self-bolstering books.
Humanistic scholars have been calling this the "Me
Decade." Titles like *Looking Out for Number One* and
Pulling Your Own Strings abound. Through diet or run-
ning or dressing or *More Joy of Sex,* the hollow people try
to dispel the stifling sense of being nobody in a world
without meaning. Whether these well advertised and often
illustrated self-help volumes deliver what they promise is
hard to discover, but the sales of ever more enticing titles
go flooding on. Along with all the searching for personality potentials, religious books also circulate by the scores
of millions. If everyone in this machine age were happy
worshipping electronics and technology, could there be a
best seller titled *I've Got to Talk to Somebody, God?*

The non-reading desolate of the seventies gorge on
audio-visual excitement: monsters, horror, sex, and violent
crime. Advertisements splash with such words as blood-
curdling, bawdy, provocative, outspokenly adult. Theatre,
cinema, TV series and newscasts, magazines, newspapers
and radio fill the days and nights with outrageously debas-
ing stimuli. And when merely seeing and hearing about
these atrocities loses its punch, the doing of them begins.

Doing, doing in person, provides the antidote to desolation. Random violence flares like forest fires. People, feeling destroyed, are bent on destroying others. Middle class whites, illiterate minorities, children between nine and twenty, pimps and gangsters brazenly outwit the police. The aged and poor are stabbed for their food money. Even the affluent brutalize their toddlers, beat wife or mistress, set fire to multifamily tenements, butcher their competitors and stuff the bleeding pieces into garbage cans. When they make sirens scream and buildings collapse, they can say, "See, I'm somebody! I can prove it! Blood, fire, rape, murder, bombs!" They gloat when headlines and newscasts blare forth their prowess. And for days thereafter, these 'events' are redescribed, kept vividly alive in the minds of still others who are uprooted, homeless and desperate.

No one escapes. Not even determined optimists who view only 'worthwhile' programs, can evade alarming statistics about famine, pollution and wars. In fact, serious programs center precisely on crises at home and abroad. Page-long editorials and huge cartoons sell disenchantment. High government officials publicly accuse one another of corruption and argue about which nation or how many enemy nations can "strike first" with megabombs. "Dangerous toys" thinks Tom. "Some fool pushes the wrong button, and we blow up. Extinction, like the dinosaurs."

Men of the so-called pure sciences are fortunately not that lost and desolate. For more than a century they have had exciting goals—pursuing the ever more astonishing truth, facts and laws about creation and how it happened. At thousands of citadels of learning, teams of scientists, highly respected and well funded, probe deep into the microcosms and far out to the edges of the macrocosm. Their findings, amazing as they are, profit the average man very little, however, for they are reported in technical journals beyond the understanding of even educated laymen. Although scientists themselves are not uprooted, many now openly admit that materialism and runaway technology have increased, rather than alleviated, humanity's problems.

In *Future Shock* Alvin Toffler studies today's rate of environmental change and mankind's inability to cope with it: "Here, then, is a pressing intellectual agenda for the social and physical sciences. We have taught ourselves to create and combine the most powerful of technologies. We have not taken pains to learn about their consequences. Today these consequences threaten to destroy us. We must learn, and learn fast . . . Faced with the power to alter the gene, to create new species, to populate the planets or depopulate the earth, man must now assume conscious control of evolution itself . . . shaping tomorrow to human need."

"Shaping tomorrow to human need" is also the goal of Abraham Maslow's humanistic psychology which calls for a "New World View," "a change of basic thinking along the total front of man's endeavors, a potential change in every social institution . . . a new philosophy of science, of education, of religion, of psychotherapy, of politics, of economics, etc., etc., etc."

Man, from his earliest beginnings has shaped his tomorrows to meet his close-in needs. Adam and Eve did it by eating of the Tree. In consequence they were 'banished,' uprooted, and had to shape a new tomorrow. But for aeons man has survived his uprootings, has ceased to be merely an animal enduring what came his way, has evolved into a *self*, choosing, planning, facing ever new wildernesses. Dawn man, remembering how he and his woman played with their weanling in the noonday sun, longed even at dark for that warmth and joy—invented fire. Riding down stream on a slippery log, he imagined hollowing it out—behold, a boat. On land he rolled his boat uphill by placing logs under it and after centuries— the wheel. Always a Somewhat within him kept reaching, slowly grasping, then reaching again, for new triumphant tomorrows. Always he was proud of his imaginings, loved his inventions and made them do his bidding.

But modern man's inventions have ceased to do his bidding; they have taken command, uprooted him. Not his human needs, not his private joys, but the demands of behemoth technology and government must be met. And so the Somewhat has risen in protest, refuses to be crushed among the armored tanks of the Machine Age.

Chapter Two

MAN THE HUMAN, INVENTOR OF GODS

The current endangerment of the human species is being quite generally recognized—many are the doomsayers—but diversely diagnosed. Causes mentioned are: greed and lust, wealth, poverty, ignorance, intellectualism, original sin, heathenism and/or innate animal aggressiveness. All these, no doubt, are factors. The hard sciences maintain that man, being the most intellectual mammal known, should be able to cope with the Machine Age; by more intellect, more learning, he must be taught that this is the best of all possible worlds. But the *human* sciences—education, anthropology and psychology—are now discovering that the superorganizationalism that man has set up as his environment is incompatible with a basic element in his humanness.

Scholars like Sir James Frazer and Joseph Campbell have presented the world with evidence that man has a subtle extra ingredient which non-humans, no matter how teachable, do not have—not the beaver who cleverly builds dams, not the dolphin who can fasten explosives to underwater objects, not the chimpanzee who manipulates a picture computer. *Genus homo,* having ventured to leave his tree-top habitat, defenseless against prowling carnivores, obviously needed to re-orient himself, needed somehow to explain why and how he was different. By instinct he knew some inborn ways of surviving, but in his new environment he needed to choose and plan, to image new inter-speci-al ways. Neighbors physically equipped to destroy him and yet essential to his very existence, needed to be kept friendly, be propitiated. They had value and meaning, deserved respect. In such a scary, lonely life a trait specific to humankind, a concept of relatedness, obligation, even sacredness was born.

In this new habitat with so many overlapping territories, each with its dominant male and its pecking order, was there not, this one-time ape must have wondered, an even more dominant male to set the pattern? Flocks of birds had leaders, herds of camels had leaders; could there not be a Topmost, a colossal Authority, for *all* species? Perhaps the first inkling of such an All Mighty came to him when the glory of a rainbow enchanted him, lifted him into a magic world. Perhaps like a sunrise touching all with radiance, the answer to his puzzlings slowly dawned on him.

Perhaps, like a man possessed, he suddenly was sure that of course there was a Leader of all leaders, a Chieftain of all chieftains, a highest Commander over land and sea and man and beast. Of course! Irradiated, he raced to his neighbor families and mimed his ecstasy. As if by spontaneous combustion, man, woman, and child were also aflame. Suddenly they all knew that a Somewhat, greater than their most formidable enemy, higher than the heavens, ruled *all* life.

"His face must be as big as the tallest man!" They cut a tree, painted a huge face on it, lifted it high amid their cluster of huts. Jubilant, they pranced and danced, orgied around it, all of them, until they were exhausted but safe and protected. Another face, a giant mask for the tribesman who could be agent of the Almighty, translating into

gesture and familiar sounds, a dominant human male, sha-
man, priest. This was more important even than mating
rituals, this was community sacredness.

Just how and where such imagings began, the anthro-
pologists cannot tell; ecstasies leave no fossil traces. But
actual skeletal remains, groupings of artifacts, graves and
massive sanctuary caves do conclusively prove that dawn
man envisaged a central, all-commanding Somewhat to be
venerated. In paying homage to that Somewhat it was
honor and glory to give one's labor, one's first-born, one's
own life. Depending on geographic conditions and on the
tribe's evolutionary level, God-images varied enormously,
but always the God-story was *lived out;* what instinct is for
the groundhog, the God-notion was for early man. In his
book *Human Destiny* Lecomte du Noüy stated this human
necessity thus:

"It is not the image of God that proves God,
It is the effort we make to create that image."

(Italics by LdN)

Fifty thousand years ago primitive hunters painted their
notions of God, food, fertility and prowess on cave walls.
For the extra-devout they dug long narrow passages to inner sanctuaries. Nomadic or settled on arable land,
anthropos created and imaged not only a plausible Most
High, but also an ethical framework, a mythos, which tied
him in with that Most High. When *anthropos* became
homo sapiens, he changed the name mythos to religion;
this was an apt change, for does not the word religion,
from the Latin *ligare,* mean being tied-in? The word religion, as also *liga*ture, ob*liga*tion, *leag*ue and a*lign*ment,
literally signifies belonging. Whether the name be myth or
religion, the need to belong is neither heathen nor Jewish
nor Christian; it is universally human.

Modern man's endangerment, aside from the external

hazards of someone's pushing the wrong button, ecological contamination or violent crime, is due to his being deprived in the area of this universal need, this sacredness. His highest priority during thousands of generations has, in the span of little more than a hundred years, been declared irrelevant. The pace of external change has been so rapid that today only octogenarians clearly remember gaslit rooms, horse-drawn carriages and the beginnings of telephone, radio and television.

But inner change does not happen that quickly; deep non-conscious trends and aspirations, encoded in the psyche, are long-lived and demand a semblance of satisfaction. How deeply embedded man's past is in his unconscious only modern psychiatry can appraise. Carl Jung's twentieth century explorations of the individual and the collective unconscious have revealed that drives and patterns born when man was barely hominid remain dynamic in the core of the psyche and resist radical repression. Like growth rings in the tree trunk, the unconscious is built, culture by culture. Unforgotten are the fears and darings of each era, the uprootings and modifications in its God-story. However different the language and ritual, the theme has always been—and remains—"unless I belong to my God-story, I am dissolved into nothingness."

For the Judeo-Christian world the variations upon this single theme which are most pertinent began about 4000 B.C. A race now known as the Sumerians lived in Mesopotamia, the fertile valley between the Tigris and Euphrates Rivers, named in Genesis as the location of the Garden of Eden. Here market towns grew into great cities, supported not only by agriculture but by commerce which moved along the Fertile Crescent, an ancient trade route connecting India and Egypt. This 'Garden' was also accessible by sail through the Persian Gulf or the Red Sea.

The alluvial soil of Mesopotamia yielded rich finds to modern archeologists, revealing that there the priests had remarkably clear knowledge of mathematics and astronomy and were full-time, professionally strict, temple potentates. They based the God-story on the zodiac—sun, moon and five known planets—and saw to it that the secular order of their city states became an imitation of the heavenly system. The ceremonial lives of royalty, the architecture of cities, and the activities of the citizenry were designed to be in accord with the movements of the celestial bodies. King and queen, like sun and moon, were central as was the sacred shrine atop the ziggurat—a man-made hill of dried clay blocks—which symbolized the height where the union of earthly and heavenly powers is consummated.

The myth of the Sumerian era demanded large-scale human sacrifice. The priesthood, by astrological calculations, determined when king, queen and their entire retinue were to be collectively entombed. This fact was discovered by a British archeologist in the year 1926. He excavated several such royal catacombs in the vicinity of Ur, birthplace of Abraham, a city near the delta of the Tigris and Euphrates Rivers. The archeologist was amazed at what he found, and he wrote long letters home giving detailed descriptions.

Long underground ramps, he wrote, led to brick enclosed vaults on two different levels where king and queen were ensconced. Along the ramps lay bedaggered bodyguards, charioteers with gold-encrusted chariots, oxen and asses harnessed to their wagons, all in perfect formation. The king in his elaborate chamber had three attendants and all were protected by some sixty persons in the death pit. The queen had only two ladies in waiting at her side as she lay on her bier covered from collar to waist with necklaces of semiprecious stones. She wore a huge headdress and others were in reserve. A harpist, gold-crowned, was provided; she lay across her wooden harp of which only the gold and lapis decorations remained. No signs of reluctance or coercion. All had obviously volunteered their lives in sacred ritual. The pageant was then covered with layers of earth heavy enough to crush skulls and helmets. For thousands of years no one except occasional thieves had profaned this mass burial.

At the Egyptian end of the Fertile Crescent the Myth and culture of Mesopotamia gradually intermingled with indigenous Nile legends of Horus, Isis and Osiris. Trade carried not only merchandise but new God-stories, arts and ways of living. Record keeping, the calendar of 360-plus-five special days, mathematics and hierarchical practices on priestly and kingship levels appeared wherever camel, ass, ox, wheel or sail could reach. The pyramids, oriented like the ziggurat to the four points of the compass, became the sumptuous resting places for pharaoh kings. Instead of making wedge-shaped marks in moist clay tablets, the Egyptians cut pictographs in sandstone walls. As in India and Mesopotamia, certain animals were held sacred and honored with statues of gold and precious stone.

Out of the pomp and idolatry of Sumerian culture there issued, about 1800 B.C., a very different myth. A man called Abram, aged seventy-five and childless, heard a voice which told him to leave the land of his fathers and go with wife and nephew Lot, into the simplicity of nature. Abram's decision to heed the voice, reject the old story and build a new one, foreshadows modern man's dilemma. The story growing out of this decision, will be studied in greater detail as the development of Western man's consciousness continues.

Next, chronologically, came Greek mythology. A language of great precision and beauty had already developed when Homer, about 800 B.C., wrote his immortal epics. Here the concept of divinity involved no earthly kings, and even the priesthood seemed to be less dominant than along the Fertile Crescent. The Greek gods were a super-human family living not on a ziggurat, but atop Mount Olympus; Zeus had a wife and offspring, all depicted in statuary as superb human forms. Each member of the Olympian family had jurisdiction over certain aspects of human life—wisdom, fertility, hunting, speed, cunning—somewhat like the patron saints in Catholicism. The names of the known planets were used, but the government of Greek city states was not, as in Sumeria, an imitation of the celestial system. These gods spoke through priestesses at sacred oracles, received seasonal adulation in massive temples, protected deserving persons, punished sinners, and occasionally had progeny with ordinary humans.

The Romans, centuries later, adopted the Greek gods, merely renaming them. When their empire grew so large as to be unmanageable, they demanded, not worship of gods, but worship of the ruling caesars. Failure to do this brought to martyrdom thousands of early Christians. In many cases that martyrdom, too, was taken to be a salvation-earning human sacrifice. Elaine Pagels' book *The Gnostic Gospels* sheds light on the Orthodox versus Gnostic Christian attitudes towards persecution. Could the still lingering idea, "'Tis noble to suffer" stem from those days?

Even so short an account reveals that from before the time of agriculture, man built a story, a cosmology, and prescribed a system of worship, and he tied his own worth to participation in that system. Since this imprint lies so deep in the unconscious, Tom and his many counterparts cannot rationally explain why they feel so empty and deprived. Perhaps in daughter Jane, because of her adolescence, the need to belong to a Somewhat is more explosive than in her adult parents, so she has been joining 'peer groups,' gangs and cults. Without knowing it today's young and old alike are suffering withdrawal from an elemental value system. Their unconscious rebels against being easily replaceable links between anonymous institutions and their products. Can they now, so desperately cut off from the Anchor of their selfness, cease repudiating the 'outdated' Story and begin trying to understand a more evolved belongingness?

Of this situation Maslow wrote that mankind "is between old value systems which did not work and new ones not yet born. . . . We need a validated, usable system of human values that we can believe in and devote ourselves to . . . ''

The need is too urgent to await the coming of a lone, illumined "Christos" whose ardent followers, over three centuries, managed to set up a system which has served middling well until now. Unfortunately, the churchmen have done little to maintain their system's credibility. Man has ventured too far, eating of the knowledge of atoms, organs, and organisms, the knowledge of beast and man, of suns, whirling planets, and of machines, to get him there. Western man is in a new wilderness. Now scientists must take leadership and present man with a new Story, a multidimensional system, academically *and* humanly valid, by which man can once more find a way out of the wilderness, a way back to partnership with what he once called God.

Chapter Three

THE SURVIVAL TEAM

Scientists, acting as one composite entity, are the only ones qualified to mobilize society for comprehensive change. Toffler warns that we need more and more "future-oriented think tanks." Scientists are the only ones trained to explore beyond known boundaries, to think on things abstract, to analyze and verify the interconnectedness of things once considered disparate. Scientists have the esteem of industry, education and agriculture. Workers, blue collar as well as white collar, welcome scientific improvements. The media are eager to proclaim new breakthroughs.

Biophysicist John R. Platt, in his 1969 book *Projections for Survival,* sets up time tables for solving the most urgent crises of this era. The time during which he estimated there was a fifty-fifty chance of outliving the crises has almost elapsed. So much more reason to follow his plan for an all-science task force: one huge interdisciplinary Survival Team of humanity-minded scientists. Having in the past forged ahead in hundreds of divergent directions, having pierced into the submicroscopic and reached outward to the ballooning galaxies, they must now all focus on one central target—that bundle of physical, chemical and psychic intangibles, their next of kin, man.

In a monumental effort scientists must now submerge the professional ego, descend from the ivory tower, and build their vast store of information into one thoroughly integrated wisdom. That wisdom must present an updated World View suitable for the layman in his need for a validated value system. The task will be threefold:

(a) to explore and agree on a comprehensive plan for humanizing current socio-economic patterns.

(b) to formulate a cosmology which plausibly interprets and expands upon traditional religion.

(c) to win the enthusiasm of business, academe and the uprooted common man.

The Team's first step will be to spread out from the sharply defined areas of research they have been pursuing and to study where the worst incompatibilities lie. To discover how monolithic institutions can release their octopus hold on the average man, a large number of scientists must be willing to enter the lay world, to listen openmindedly and observe creatively. Talented public relations persons will have to elicit from the tycoons of business, education and government, their opinions of possible modifications. They will confront highly paid 'development personnel' who resent tampering with their plans. However difficult, the Team's work must be carried on with unrelenting investigation and unrelenting reform.

While step (a) is being carried on among lay persons administering the socio-economic environment, the Team must, in professional consultation, perform an even more formidable task. A new cosmology sketching out a unified theory of Reality must be formulated. It must show the continuous interacting of energy, mass and law. What the Myth did for dawn man the new cosmology must do for today's man. It must be abstract enough for the precision-minded scientist and yet image-able enough for the empty-hearted, deprived-of-his-God layman. This new frame of reference must be a composite of all theories postulated by the various disciplines, a unified model of physical, mental, emotional and psychic forces interpenetrating one another like concentric spheres in perpetual motion.

Einstein is said to have felt that the cosmic religious experience is the strongest and noblest mainspring of scientific research. If this is so for scientists in general, then each member of the Team ought to understand that his fellow man's inherited religious unconscious will respond to a new-found empirical value system. The new cosmology must provide that every individual, every physical and non-physical particle actually is tied-in, aligned with, in alliance with, the Universe of universes. This cosmic panorama must indicate where, in the huge span between atom and galaxy, the despairing human of today stands. It must disprove the notion that the cosmos is a loose collection of phenomena whirling machine-like in space; it must establish that, on the contrary, the cosmos is a highly sensitive organism in which all minute groupings of organisms serve in what is undeniably an orderly process of evolution. The Team must validate for every Tom, Jane and Sally that the highest commitment of humankind is indispensable if that evolution is to continue on the planet earth.

The third step in the Team's survival project lies in an area equally unfamiliar to scientists—that of widespread communication. The unitive cosmology, the commonsense non-church and yet awe-inspiring Story must be publicized. With ever renewed ingenuity in public relations, every old and every innovative method must be marshalled to proclaim it with maximum eclat. It must be blazoned forth as a heroic prophecy of resurrection from the deadness of this age.

This communication must do more than merely inform, it must inspire. Whereas the customary research terminology inspires scientists engaged in similar disciplines, is excellent for technical journals and can be fed into computers, such purely factual language misses this Team's target, the average uprooted private soul. To revive that soul's hope and invite his commitment one must address his *feelings,* spark his imagination and free his repressed inwardness.

To mix objective facts with subjective overtones is apparently becoming acceptable scholastically. Three examples of such presentations are recent works by eminent scientists in diverse fields: Julian Huxley's 1956 *Religion Without Revelation,* Joseph Campbell's 1969 *Masks of God* and Harlow Shapley's 1967 *Beyond the Observatory.* The last named Harvard astronomer, in a chapter titled "Life and Hope," asks for the abandonment of a one-planet religion and a one-planet deity. Scientist though he is, he calls for revised philosophies and religions, for an assemblage of ideals and a modern program for personal and societal life. Shapley goes beyond Albert Schweitzer's "reverence for life" and insists that not only life, but the wonder of the entire natural world be recognized and reverenced. Indeed, he pleads for man to avow reverence for all that is touched by cosmic evolution—especially for that which "was in the beginning" when "the earth was without form and void," namely, Existence Itself. Can Existence Itself be anything other than a more-than-one-planet deity?

In two-stranded language such as this the Survival Team must sketch out a new world view, a new belief-system which combines fact with the legacies of myth and religion. An edifice of truth with far-reaching dimensions must be outlined. This panorama must become an expanded Homeland, evoking wonder and devotion. Though still unfinished, it must be rich in promise. It must show that man has overcome countless uprootings. It must inspire man to seek ever more enlightenment, to realize that he "belongs." It must start him on a crusade for the survival of the worshipper, the dreamer and doer.

In triumphant fortissimo all media must tell of the Team's new cosmology. The breakthrough must strike the world with an impact greater than that of the atomic bomb or the first moon landing. Seminars at colleges, museums and libraries, PTA, AA, Yoga and TM groups must spread the revised, non-theological, non-doctrinal Story of *homo sapiens*. For every last frustated Tom, Jane and Sally the Team's new cosmic panorama must come with the force of a conversion experience such as those of St. Paul and St. Francis.

So much for the work of the Survival Team, the humanizing of social conditions, the formulating and publicizing of a new world view. Each anguished private citizen must now do what he can to orient himself in the new environment and utilize it according to the "new program for life." Of course he must carefully survey the friendlier field, but it is far more important that he survey his inherited value systems and reconcile them with the vast dimensions of the "revised ideals" now opening for him. No Team, no group, only each person within himself can do this. With patience and an open mind modern man must now think and feel his way into becoming a creative partner in the quest for humanity's common good.

Chapter Four

SURVEYING THE SELF

As stated, more than the environment needs to be surveyed. Each private self must get his bearings, liberate himself from desperation and learn to become a comprehending participant in the Team's new cosmic Oneness. In acquainting himself with the deep levels of his consciousness he will have to face up to the fact that he is more than a neatly severed, one-generation slice of his entireness. He consists instead of countless physical, emotional, mental and spiritual ingredients, intermixed throughout the churnings of history into a dynamic composite of reactions. To look with hindsight at these complexities, will help him to grow comfortably into the Team's improved social habitat.

For Western man a convenient starting point for this self-survey is Abram's breakaway from Babylon, the royal city of Mesopotamia. The Old Testament of the Judeo-Christian Bible vividly portrays his inborn aptitudes and failings, ideals and habits. It tells of his experience during a childhood lasting more than a hundred generations. It is his early biography, his psychological genealogy. Whether the religious doctrines of these writings are fervently endorsed, condescendingly tolerated or vehemently rejected, their significance cannot be denied. The Old Testament has been a blessed stronghold in millions of human crises.

But it is a factor not just occasionally; it is a source book for the study of mankind's evolving consciousness. It tells of uprootedness, of the need to 'belong,' and the disciplines invented to prevent backslidings. The parallel with today's predicament cannot be ignored.

The Abram families, setting forth with kith and kin, household possessions plus sheep and cattle, could not well carry bits of moist clay on which to record their doings and remember their identity. Instead they memorized and kept retelling the names and events of their journeyings. Their names were not chosen hit or miss: root syllables were combined to carry meanings. The names of heroes and sacred places always included the God-syllable *el* or *iah*. Beth*el,* where the first altar was built, meant "House of God," Immanu*el* meant "God within." Jerem*iah,* Isa*iah* and Ezek*iel* were important prophets. *Eli̇jah* had both syllables, perhaps for extra authority.

Names were changed when a person's character or destiny changed. When, for instance, Abram complained to the Voice that he was old and childless, his name was changed to Abraham, meaning "Father of a Nation." When his quarrelsome, over-aged wife Sarai bore him a son—to be named Isaac, "Laughter"—her name became Sarah, "Noble Woman." When Jacob was to confront his brother Esau whom he had betrayed of his birthright, he wrestled with his conscience—a man angel—until that angel blessed him and changed his name to Israel, meaning "Prince with God." By everlasting repetition of those meaning-packed names, the many Israelite generations maintained their sense of identity and belongingness.

In those days, as today, inherited tendencies and habits were not suddenly erased. The practice of human sacrifice, deeply ingrained as a way of worship, persisted. The testing of Abraham (Gen. 22:1–18) is an example. When the

Voice commanded that Isaac, his beloved son so miraculously born, become a burnt offering, father Abraham started a three day trip to the appointed place. Isaac, having carried the wood and helped build the altar, was bound and laid thereon. Fire was at hand. Knife uplifted, Abraham again heard the Voice. This time it halted the killing. Having proven his faith in and fear of his God, Abraham was instructed to sacrifice a ram which stood in a nearby thicket.

That incident marked the end of human sacrifice in Judaism, but the offering up of animals continued to play an important role. In all Old Testament ritual, especially for absolution of sin, certain numbers of certain animals were sacrificed in certain ways. Tithing and paying for masses to be said for the afflicted are relics of these practices which persist to this day.

The Abraham families—soon enough they were a multitude—suffered hardships and family feuds. Jacob's favorite son Joseph, the dreamer and interpreter of dreams, was so envied by his brothers that they schemed to destroy him. But this wearer of the coat of many colors, "Imagination," was able to render misfortune into good fortune by becoming the Egyptian Pharaoh's advisor. Moreover he requited the betrayal by his eleven brothers with great benevolence. He induced the Pharaoh to send food to the starving tribes and later to provide fertile land whereon they could settle.

After some four hundred years, however, times had changed, and the Israelites found themselves cruelly enslaved. One of them, later named Moses, struck down one of the taskmasters and fled for his life to Sinai. There, while tending sheep on Mt. Horeb, he heard the Voice speaking from a bush which was aflame but not consumed. The Voice charged him to return to Egypt and draw his people out of bondage. Reluctant to attempt such a mighty task, Moses begged to be excused, but the Voice—now identifying Itself as "God of Abraham" and the "I AM"—persuaded him that he, too, could do "signs and wonders." Finally, promised divine help, he and Aaron set forth to convert the Pharaoh and free the Israelites. It took ten hideous plagues which tormented the Egyptians while sparing the Hebrews, and many other miracles, plus the dividing of the Red Sea, to free the Jews dry-shod and drown the pursuing Egyptians.

Again they were uprooted, again in new territory. Though as if by magic they had manna to eat, protests, "murmurings" and backslidings soon cropped up. When they had reached the Sinai, Moses went up to the "Mountain of God" to receive more instructions. He delayed too long; the people complained and collected gold earrings out of the women's ears to be made into an idol. When Moses came down from the Mount, he found them singing, dancing and worshipping a golden Calf. Enraged, he cast out of his hands the tablets "written with the finger of God" (Ex. 31:18) and ground to a powder the unholy Calf.

Later, Moses pleaded with the Lord that he might forgive his sinning, stiffnecked people, carried up two more tablets hewn of stone, and returned after forty days, having himself written on them a new covenant about worship and the Ten Commandments. (Ex. 34:28)

These wandering tribes needed more than marvels, mighty thunderings and sparsely worded commandments; they needed images and orgiastic rituals. Soon the Voice proclaimed to Moses minute instructions for the building of a holy tabernacle constructed of certain woods, gold, silver and brass, with hangings of blue, purple and scarlet. The people brought gifts of spun linen and goat's hair. Exact specifications were given for altar, vessels, candlestick and priestly garments. This was a sanctified, tangible sanctuary with definite, prescribed ways of worship, a center where priests could control and enforce atonements, sacrifices and penalties. There were innumerable rules and taboos also, for daily hygiene, marriage practices and trade, all of which were intended to prevent further backslidings and keep the people constantly obedient to their Almighty Lawgiver.

To the Israelites the letter of the law was important. Even Moses had transgressed. During the forty year trek he had struck the rock twice, instead of once, for water. For that reason he was not to enter the Promised Land. And so, East of the Jordan, across from Jericho, he dutifully appointed Joshua to succeed him, pronounced many additional laws, made three long speeches, blessed God and the Israelites, and died. Joshua, following instructions of God exactly, maneuvered the crossing of the Jordan. Again the waters were divided. First seven priests crossed over carrying the ark of the covenant, then the armed men and the rest of the people; the remaining priests closed up the rear. All crossed over dry-shod just in time to celebrate that year's Passover. The city was circled once each day for six days with only the priests blowing trumpets, but on the seventh day Jericho was circled seven times, and at a signal all the people "shouted with a great shout." Thereupon the wall fell down flat. The people went up into the city and "utterly destroyed all that was in the city, both man and woman, young and old, and ox and sheep and ass, with the edge of the sword."

Yes, the Israelites at long last had a foot in the Promised Land. After many a misdeed and many a stoning of culprits, they managed to "slay the natives with great slaughter" and parcel out the conquered lands among the twelve Abraham tribes. For about a hundred years disputes and transgressions among them were adjudicated by travelling

judges, but then the people wanted a king, a central
earthly authority. With their God's permission Judge
Samuel appointed Saul, who was not really a great ruler.
David, the lad who felled Goliath, became Saul's succes-
sor and managed, during his long and none-too-virtuous
reign, to subdue the armies of the Philistines and start
building the temple at Jerusalem. The next king, Solomon,
finished the temple, expanded trade and established a well-
structured affluent monarchy. After almost nine hundred
years, God's covenant with Abraham seemed fulfilled: the
Israelites were indeed "a great nation."

The glory of success, however, brought on an unwhole-
some laxness. A series of wicked, even "loathsome" kings
ruled briefly. Lofty-minded prophets went unheard. Division became rampant; ten of the tribes set up a rival capital in the North, appropriating the name Israel. That left
only two tribes who kept the name Judah, "Praise Jeho-
vah," and worshipped in the temple at Jerusalem.

Next a period of mass invasions set in; Persians overran
the two kingdoms separately. The Northern kingdom fell
in 722 B.C. and Jerusalem was first sacked in 597. Ten
years later in a second onslaught the great temple was
demolished. Judah's king and some 48,000 people were
marched captive to Babylonia, the very heathen land
which, twelve hundred years earlier, Abraham had
repudiated.

There, in exile, a Jerusalem priest named Ezekiel was so
eloquent in writing and preaching that he is now often
called "The Father of Judaism." He described a series of
visions in which the Lord God gave him messages for the
Israelites. The downfall of their kingdom, he was to tell
them, was due to their having fallen into idolatrous worship. They were to repent: "From all your idols I will
cleanse you . . . I will take away the stony heart out of
your flesh . . . and I will put my spirit within you, and

cause you to walk in my statutes, and ye shall keep my judgements and do them." (Ez. 36:25–27) Ezekiel's fervor was so great that his people actually listened.

In order to prevent contamination of the sacred doctrine during the long years of exposure to heathen religions, he instituted daily orthodox worship. He even inspired other captivity priests to collect ancient scrolls telling archaic legends, folk tales and genealogies. A compendium of laws given during the wanderings was made into a single code, Leviticus. A "reformed version" of Judaic history and law from Moses to Solomon, written a century earlier, was smuggled in from Jerusalem. This book, Deuteronomy, emphasized that God—Yahveh—alone was God, to be worshipped at Jerusalem only, and that social morality must be combined with a purified worship system.

After seventy years in exile the Hebrews were allowed to return home. Zealously, throughout twenty years they worked at rebuilding their temple. By the time it was finished, the priests of that generation, largely under the help of Ezra, had put together one huge scroll—the Pentateuch—later cut into five "Books of the Law." These five books are the crux of Judaism. Thirty-four ancillary books, The Prophets, came to form the authentic Old Testament, which stands to this day as the supreme law governing the outer, *and* the inner, lives of millions of moderns.

The Old Testament is not history as modern science knows history, chronologically correct and objective. These writings are the outbursts of mystics and inspired leaders committed to shepherding their people into the worship of a single, almighty, superhuman God. They reveal man's recognition of a non-physical level of his I-AM-ness, which all too often succumbs to brute nature. They blurt out how deep yearnings for worthiness alternate with greed, envy and violent aggression. They reveal

Chapter Five

THE CHRISTIANIZED SELF

The hardships of the Abraham tribes, as described in the Old Testament, are dominant in the unconscious of those who have clung to Judaism. But the influences of those centuries also linger in the unconscious of those who gradually began following the precepts of the controversial young Rabbi Jesus, the Man of Galilee. His life and the birthing of Christianity form the context of the New Testament. Since 325 A.D. these twin testaments have been expounded to Christians on every holy day from every pulpit in the Western world. They were the one continuing law and authority uniting the lowest and the highest, sanctifying the most momentous crises and putting the stamp of validity on births, marriages and deaths. Even for Jews, for agnostics and atheists the ancient symbolic gestures and prejudices live on dynamically, only thinly veneered-over, in the unconscious.

Though the Christian religion was born of the Judaic and both center their worship on one, and *only* one God, there are significant differences in the way the texts came to be. The Israelite prophets poured out their messages long before there was a written language. When scribes finally learned to make Aramaic symbols with ink on dried skins or papyrus, they had to rely on oral versions memorized by successive generations. Of course, some of the later prophets did their own inscribing and later still the scattered remnants of their writings were pieced together. When the Pentateuch was formally compiled, the old wordings were too sacred to be changed.

The New Testament text, on the other hand, was set down by educated believers, in language more evolved by a thousand years. They wrote what they remembered, or their elders reported what they had personally seen.

The Old Testament covers eighteen warring centuries of nomadic life during which countless mystics and reformers fought to establish a One-God religion; the New Testament begins with that One-God religion as it was understood by a single great teacher. In the one "The Law" evolved; in the other that law was interpreted by a more articulate mystic. The Old commanded rules of obedience and conduct; the New pleaded for worshipful motivation.

Since the four Gospels, the main accounts of this great teacher's life, were set down at long intervals, there are variations between them. It seems best to give a composite story and later to note differences in texts. Jesus was born when Carpenter Joseph of Galilee and his young wife Mary neared Jerusalem to be counted in the Roman census. The date, astronomers calculate, was the year when a conjunction of heavenly bodies brightened the sky over Judea. Twelve years later that same family went to Jerusalem again, this time to celebrate the Passover feast; son Jesus—the name means 'savior' or 'deliverer'—tarried three days in the temple listening to discussions between the priests.

Jesus is mentioned again when, at age thirty, he stood among the crowds attracted by an itinerant reformer named John. Seeing Jesus in line for baptism, John hesitated, saying he had a strong feeling that here, indeed, was the Messiah, the long expected deliverer of the Jews. But Jesus insisted on baptism and was immersed. The crowd claimed that as he stepped out of the Jordan a beam of light shaped like a dove descended upon Jesus' head and a Voice thundered, "This is my beloved son in whom I am well pleased." All four Gospels tell of this incident.

Jesus "straightway" went into the wilderness and fasted forty days. Possibly he felt that if indeed he was 'called' he wanted to be certain that he would be strong enough to use his power not for wealth, possessions or glory, but to serve God only. On returning to Galilee he gathered about him twelve men who believed, as John the Baptist did, that he really was the Messiah, Son of God. Wherever he went with these twelve, multitudes gathered to hear him, touch his garment and be healed.

In less than three years he was so popular that the temple priests felt their authority threatened. This young Unknown did such outrageous things as heal a withered arm on a Sabbath. He even dared to declare that the Sabbath was made for man, not otherwise; worst of all, when Passover crowds filled Jerusalem he cast the moneychangers out of the temple and overturned the tables where sacrificial animals were sold. Often tested and heckled by priestly 'lawyers,' Jesus was well aware that "they sought how they could destroy him." The rich were also quick to denounce him for eating with the lower classes, for not stoning an adulteress and for not praying ostentatiously on street corners as they did. He realized that he and his followers could not prevail against those who pretended to obey the letter of the Law while they violated the spirit of it. Facing the fact that his words and deeds would soon be forgotten if he were made quietly to disappear, he continued to defy the hecklers and challenge their machinations. He decided that if need be he would give up his physical life so that his spiritual message might live. But he was determined that his death must be a dramatic climax, an unforgettable confirmation of his message in life.

Knowing that the expulsion of the moneychangers and what is now known as the 'Triumphal Entry' had angered the temple priests, Jesus realized that his end was imminent. At the Passover meal he gave his last sermon, prayed for the Twelve and reassured them that the Father would send "The Spirit of Truth" to comfort them. Saddened, he went apart and prayed for strength to go through with the ordeal. He had been right about the imminence of his sacrifice, for on that very night the high priests brought on the climax. At a signal from Judas they sent a mob of armed men to get the "imposter" by night into the council chamber. Paid witnesses testified that he was a blasphemer. Jesus was pronounced guilty.

On the next day came the drama that was to make him and his message unforgettable. He was dragged through the streets to the hall of Pilate, the Roman Governor. There priest and public taunted him about the claim that he was Messiah, and called him instead the self-appointed "King of the Jews." Pilate, thus goaded, ordered crucifixion.

Huge crowds celebrating Passover in Jerusalem avidly followed the Roman soldiers who marched Jesus and two thieves to "Golgotha, which is to say, a place of a skull." They gaped while the three were nailed to their crosses, and stayed on to watch the guards make sure that all were dead. With the crucifying over and darkness approaching, only the few women who had come with Jesus from Galilee were left, desolate. They observed that a rich man, with permission of Pilate's guards, took the body of their master and placed it in a clean tomb near by. After the Sabbath one of the women returned and found the tomb empty. There and at various other times and places Jesus appeared, spoke and exhorted his disciples to go unto all nations and teach as he had taught.

The disciples, more firmly convinced than ever by the

martyrdom and the re-appearances of Jesus, made many converts in Jerusalem. They were, of course, severely harassed by the priests: Peter was imprisoned and Stephen was stoned. Saul, a member of the temple council, having heard of a crusade to be mounted in Damascus, set out to arrest more of the heretics. On the road there, however, Saul had a luminous vision, heard the voice of Jesus and was struck blind. After three days in hiding and without food he was rescued by a disciple, also in hiding and also instructed by the voice. Saul, his sight restored, was baptized and given food; he "straightway" preached in the synagogue about the Man of Galilee whom he had helped to condemn. At first he was mistrusted by both Jews and the Jerusalem disciples, but after some years he gained acceptance, was renamed Paul, and journeyed three times around the shores of the Mediterranean, founding churches. His letters to those churches were the very first written instructions in Christian doctrine. Though many of them were destroyed during the Roman persecutions, those remaining became the ten main "Epistles," a large part of the New Testament.

The disciple James manned the post in Jerusalem, but the others went forth by land and sea, to spread the teaching of Jesus throughout the vast Greco-Roman Empire. They were a scattered few in an agglomeration of ethnically and religiously diverse peoples. Fortunately, the official Greek language contained the word *Christos,* which served well to convey the Hebrew concept of Messiah, Savior, Deliverer. Were not those far-flung populations, so long crushed under Roman arrogance, sorely in need of a Savior? The word caught on. Christ and Christianity were the new names of hope and courage. A new Myth, a new Story united them in their misery—the oppressed natives and the persecuted Christians.

Peter, the disciple who had thrice denied even knowing

Jesus during the trials, was the first to work in Rome. Paul, after founding churches in small towns, though captive to the Roman army, achieved his ambition to join Peter and work with him in the imperial city. For seven years these two men, in ever increasing danger, preached in secret to their converts in the catacombs. Under Nero their end came, Paul was beheaded and Peter crucified.

By this time thirty odd years had elapsed since Jesus' last appearance. The disciples, now called apostles, were untutored men—except for Paul—ardent listeners but not necessarily good organizers. The young churches were widely scattered; communication was nonexistent except by Christian messenger. Perhaps some of the apostles carried a few scribblings they made during Jesus' sermons, sayings they personally loved; but on the whole during these decades, as in the long Babylonian exile, the true doctrine was in danger of contamination from heathen practices. Devout believers sensed that a uniform code must be found, as unshakable as the Temple Law. And lo! a beginning was made.

MARK   The first synopsis of Jesus' life was written
68–70 A.D.   in Rome. Mark, who had been secretary and
                translator for the two martyred apostles,
realized that Peter's firsthand knowledge of Jesus' ministry must not be lost to the young churches. He therefore wrote down in consecutive order what his two masters had so often dictated to him. In his account there is no mention of anything unusual about the birth, but the healings, parables and seemingly supernatural happenings are given in vivid simplicity. Mark told of Jesus' predicting his own death and resurrection, and of the Passover

farewell at which Jesus gave bread and wine to his Twelve, saying, "This is my body . . . and this is my blood of the new Testament which is shed for many." The trial, the angel in the empty tomb, the risen Jesus talking to his disciples, and the "being received up into heaven" are given only a few sentences.

MATTHEW 80–90 A.D. Approximately twenty years after Mark's first authentic Christian record, another converted Jew, pen-named Matthew, wrote a formal teaching manual. He used the Mark Gospel almost in its entirety, often verbatim, but added oral tradition concerning immaculate conception, the visit of wise men from the East, Herod's slaughter of the infants and, most importantly, what is now known as the Sermon on the Mount. This Gospel, almost double the length of Mark's, expands in dramatic detail on the scenes of trial, crucifixion and the empty tomb. Obviously Matthew intended to convince Judaic believers that Jesus was indeed the long prophesied Messiah bringing a new covenant, code or 'testament.' It was immediately accepted as the authoritative Christian document so badly needed to unify the young churches.

LUKE 90 A.D. A Greek physician named Luke became a close friend of Paul and of some other apostles; he even made missionary journeys with them. During Paul's imprisonment by the Romans, Luke began a narrative of Jesus' life, perhaps to prove that

Christianity was not anti-Rome. But after Paul's death
Luke must have done further research for this Gospel;
besides including almost all that Mark and Matthew had
written, Luke wove in parables later remembered, "signs
and wonders" rumored, and perhaps exaggerated, by people whose lives had been touched by Jesus.

This narrative is filled with lucid, gracious imagery. In it
the angel Gabriel appeared first to Elizabeth and then to
Mary, to announce the birth of sons to be born of the
Holy Ghost. John was to be the forerunner and Jesus the
"Son of God." Luke describes only briefly the "sharing
of bread and wine in remembrance of me" and the Judas
betrayal. But countless vivid vignettes tell how Jesus made
of his own short life a symbol of the all-indwellingness of
the Father.

ACTS   Luke also wrote the Book of Acts. He must
90 A.D.   have used the diary he kept while on the long
              sea journeys with Paul and other disciples.
It is the only extant record of where and when the Asiatic
churches were founded.

JOHN and   These two books are thought by Bible schol-
REVELATION   ars to be the work of the Presbyter of the
100 A.D.   Christian church at Ephesus. Revelation de-
              scribes a series of allegorical visions expe-
rienced by the author while in Roman captivity on the
Island of Patmos. The visions tell of atrocities yet to be

endured and surmounted by each of the seven oppressed young churches. The Gospel itself, written by this Presbyter after his release, is not so much a narrative as an *interpretation*; it is concerned with preserving the pure essence of Jesus' teaching. It claims to be the report of a "witness at the last supper who himself heard the last words that Jesus spoke."

In this account there is no mention of an "Immaculate Conception," instead this: "In the beginning was the Word . . . and the Word was God. All things were made by him: and without him (God) not anything was made. . . . In him (God) was life; . . . and life was the light of men." (John 1:1–4) "And the Word was made flesh and dwelt among us . . . " (John 1:14) In this Gospel events served mainly as occasions for stating the philosophy. Though the description of the last supper *does not* include the sharing of bread and wine, the sermon and prayer and the last scenes of the Dissident's life are depicted at greater length than in any one of the other three Gospels.

Modern man will do well to re-view what is left of the Dissident's teaching because, for the last two-thousand years it has been his topmost Authority. Christianity's first spokesman sought to change by *modifying* instead of destroying "with great slaughter." He preached interpretation, understanding and compassion. Though he had matured beyond old harshness and division, he did not scrap the old, he sought to expand it and see its deeper meaning. The lessons he taught were the same two ancient and eternal ones, but for him the two commandments

were one. To be unmindful of God Within was the sin
Jesus gave his life to correct.

The apostles, despite their ardor, were not ready to
grasp so mature an idea. Nor was the Western world
ready. On the contrary, Christianity, as it came to be
structured three centuries later, was as harsh, hierarchical
and unforgiving as Judaism had been. That rigidity, as will
be seen in further self-surveying, persists to this very day
in Western man's unconscious.

Chapter Six

GROWING PAINS

By the beginning of the second century there were, at long last, authentic stories of Jesus' life. They served as a unifying influence and yet each little church had its own battles to fight. There was a group who claimed to have *Gnosis*—the knowing—of what Jesus really meant, a mystical, spiritual interpretation. They were called heretics by the "Orthodox" churches whose bishops claimed to be in the direct line of succession of one who had communed with the "resurrected Jesus."

Only a tightly knit authority could have survived the turmoil of those days between Roman, heathen, and Gnostic. The bishops saw to it that there was indeed an organization and an authoritarian dogma, word for word literally true. This definitive movement grew, held meetings in secret, even managed to set up schools in which to spread the good news of the Deliverer. In fact, when Constantine became Emperor, he realized that among his crumbling domain the Christians gave him least trouble. He soon made a break with precedent and, by the Edict of Milan, legalized Christianity. When, after twelve years of being legally accepted, the bishops still bickered and played politics, Constantine demanded that they all come to Nicaea and unite under one "charter." They came, some 1800 of them. Constantine, sitting on a golden throne in their midst, presided over their stormy sessions. After twenty-nine days they agreed upon which books should be included in the Bible. The Nicene Creed stems from those meetings.

Suddenly the vast lands from India to Britain in which, since the crucifixion, Roman generals had wielded unholy power became the Holy *Christian* Empire with an Emperor and two popes, one in Rome and one in the East. Suddenly there was a new calendar which started with the year of Jesus' birth. Thus in the year 325 *Anno Domini,* suddenly the Christians were in command.

But the recognition of Christianity, the joining of church and state ennobled neither, nor did it bring peace and happiness. The Dark Ages were upon Europe. Hordes of pagans, Huns, Goths and Franks, overran the land. They laid waste to enormous areas, demolished the splendors of imperial edifices, made a shambles of organized life. Adding to the chaos, famines and plagues decimated the population. In the East there were also invasions. There the popes could maintain military command and church dominion, but in 638 of the new calendar, they lost to the armies of Muhammad and gave up all of Palestine, Northern Africa and Spain. Fortunately, these Muslim conquerors still permitted Christian pilgrims to visit Jerusalem, the city holy to both.

Back in Europe, natives and invaders gradually mingled; having the same needs—food and shelter—they became neighborly. Local priests baptized the new-born, tended the dying and buried the dead. Monasteries became islands of worship and service to the human soul. For temporal protection small groups clustered together under a nearby colonizing knight who paid a few soldiers and kept enough serfs to do the farming and tend the castle. As these feudal lordlings expanded their holdings, they sought the support of upper echelon clergy; the clergy also found it convenient to have the cooperation of a militarily strong lord.

Such a strong lord was one Charles, who by 771 had consolidated several disparate racial groups of Central Europe into a Frankish kingdom after the tradition of ancient Rome. Like the Caesars, he forced his religion on all he conquered. Even Christian adults had to renew their vows. Anyone refusing baptism was put to death. His soldiers subdued the troublesome Lombards, and he set up a kingdom in Italy. Pope Leo III, taking office in 795, decided that this Charles would be a useful ally to a Church regime which had little prestige. A strategic moment came on Christmas Day in the year 800. After high mass in St. Peter's Basilica, Leo clapped a bejewelled crown on the head of this desirable partner and pronounced him Carolus Magnus, Emperor Augustus of the Holy Roman Empire.

Charles the Great lived up to expectations. Though not erudite, he was energetic, able and intelligent enough to surround himself with learned men; he studied Jerome's Latin Bible—or had it read to him—and loved what he knew of it. He founded schools and monasteries, imported architects to design and build cathedrals. Even the Byzantine popes began once more to respect their Western counterparts.

But the fruitful partnership fell apart soon after Charlemagne's death. Intrigues and private wars reduced the Frankish section to a patchwork of dukedoms. Greed, violence and dissolute living were rife in both church and state. By 962 a Saxon king, Otto the Great, held sway over what is now Germany and Italy. He found it necessary to depose for treason the pope who had crowned him. He and his two successors did their best to restore decency and dignity to the joint empire, but during these times it was the character—noble or corrupt—of the reigning personality which determined the strength and reliability of papacy and government. Already plagued with internal turmoil, Europe was swept again by waves of non-Christian invaders. Norsemen, having learned to sail the seas and rivers, penetrated south and eastward to the Caspian; Magyars ravaged westward from South Russia. Thus for two hundred years since Charlemagne's rule Europe was reduced by random battlings to a jumble of fragmented territories and jurisdictions.

At that low point the Roman pope received a distress call from his rival, the Eastern patriarch. He, too, was troubled with invaders. His armies, sorely drained by keeping the warlike Muslims out of Asia Minor itself, were now being threatened by the savage Turks. They had already conquered the comparatively amiable Muslims and were blocking access to Jerusalem. Here was a chance, thought Urban II in Rome, to swallow up the Byzantine regime and meanwhile unify Europe. United in one purpose and passion, he fantasized, Christianity would punish the infidel.

With all the bishops and nobles he could muster he staged a spectacular campaign throughout Gaul and Saxony. Heartrending orations resounded from bebannered platforms imploring the "beloved and chosen of God" to rescue "the royal city at the center of the earth, now held by unclean nations." Kinglets and nobles dismounted their steeds, fell to their knees and consecrated their lives and properties to "the service of God."

Lowlier believers were enlisted by Peter the Hermit, riding an ass and carrying a huge cross. In crowded marketplaces he described the wanton destruction of the Holy Sepulcher, claiming to have seen it with his own eyes.

He and Walter the Penniless aroused tremendous fervor. Peasants, common vagrants, wayfarers and thieves joined the rich to form an Army of Haters burning to wreak vengeance "in the name of Christianity." Thousands gushed forth, unorganized, not even knowing how far the journey; for looting and stealing food along the way, most were massacred before ever reaching the Bosporus. So ignominious was the fate of that first avalanche called the People's Crusade that it was not even counted as number one of the historically acknowledged Crusades.

A year later an army of Franks, Normans and Italians, better organized, did reach Constantinople, did push on south and after a year's siege, did conquer Antioch. Most gave up there; a small group managed to capture a narrow strip along the Palestinian Coast and after a month's siege actually sacked Jerusalem. In 'holy' fervor these Christians herded the Jews into their synagogue to be burned alive and then otherwise slaughtered so many infidels that the streets ran with blood. At nightfall, having reached the Sepulcher of gentle Jesus, they joined their bloodstained hands in prayer, sobbing with the joy of being saviors of the sacred city.

But Jerusalem was soon lost to Muslim and Turkish counter-crusaders who outlasted five more Christian onslaughts. In 1228, more than a hundred years later, Frederick II, a shrewd German king, regained the city, but not for the Roman papacy! On return to Europe he chased all papal forces out of Italy, Sicily and his own German possessions. In a series of open letters he then effectually denounced the irreligion of the Church, its pride and rapacity. By 1244 the Christians had lost Jerusalem to the Sultan of Egypt and that brought about the Seventh Crusade—a dismal failure led by a French king who was taken prisoner and had to be ransomed in 1250. In all, the

Crusades caused some sixty thousand men to be slaughtered or taken into slavery. Jerusalem was still in Turkish hands.

Instead of fulfilling Pope Leo's hope and scheme for unifying feudal Europe and integrating secular with papal power, the Crusades fostered ever sharper division. Instead of combining Roman and Byzantine papacies so that together they might preach and practice the forgiveness and compassion that Jesus taught, these clashing migrations merely extended the ruthlessness they had experienced in the Mythic, Judaic and Greco-Roman persecutions. Nonetheless something had been gained through the agonies. Seeing new lands, and encountering 'barbarians' whose knowledge exceeded their own, *did* stimulate and sharpen the wits of those who survived.

Planning, failing, re-planning and following through demanded pinpointed mind activity. For Church and for the developing states money was involved. If Mediterranean seaports were closed, trade money would be missing. If the rich were no longer rich, whence the church vessels, the vestments and bejewelled mitres? The Muslims had knowledge, architecture, elegance. During those two crusade centuries the higherups learned to satisfy their worldly desires by exercising the deliberating, reasoning levels of mind. Pain or no pain, Mankind was growing into a more concentrated use of his mental endowment. Deliberation, judgement and self-criticism began to replace random emotional impulse and blind obedience to Church decree.

King Frederick's letters stuck in the minds of the princes as they squabbled among themselves. Were these Inquisitions by the Church truly Christian? Grumbling increased everywhere: "The Church is always hungry for money." The rich could buy indulgences and continue sinning while the poor did penance and had to pay besides. In those days

St. Francis of Assisi took the vow of extreme poverty and made of his own life an imitation of the life of Jesus. Thinkers complained that the Church was teaching theology, not religion; dogma, not the Sermon on the Mount. John Wycliffe, a learned English priest, dared to protest against using the Communion Service as symbol of taking into oneself the body and the blood of the Savior. To justify his protest he translated Jerome's Latin Bible into English and circulated it among his friends. Before the papal rage could climax into excommunicating him, he died a natural death. But the priests would not let him go unpunished. In 1415 at a council marking the end of a seventy year schism between French and Roman claimants to the papacy, Wycliffe's bones, exhumed after thirty years, were formally burned. At the same conclave a Czech scholar named John Huss was tried for advocating a "priestless religion." He would not recant and was burned alive. Soon thereafter came the 'Christian' burning of Joan of Arc.

But gradually even the Church's own frantic efforts to maintain domination began to wane. Travel and trade had so extended the wealth, the knowledge and the dauntlessness of feudal aristocracy that the dukes and kinglets took into their own hands the decisions about collaborating with Church potentates. Coronations, for prestige and glamor, were still practiced, but otherwise the princes had jurisdiction. Gold from abroad, transportation at home, navigation and conquest of the new world transformed the lifestyle of all but the lowliest. Even the plain burgher's skills were needed by prince and priest to build and embellish edifices commensurate with their august powers. Cathedrals, shrines and palaces for those who ruled 'by divine right' substituted for the archaic totem pole, or the temple in Jerusalem. On holy days pageantry still filled the streets. Religion in the heart was not dead; indeed, it seemed born again; for two centuries after the crusades ended religious painting and sculpture rose to a zenith.

Other crafts also prospered. Expert spinners and weavers were in demand to create textiles for sumptuous tapestries and the elaborate garments worn by lords and ladies—to say nothing of the bejewelled robes for priest and pope. When border wars began to be fought with gun powder, cannon and armor instead of with bows and arrows, more metals had to be mined, manufactured and transported. Barges for inland waterways and huge ships for trade with the Americas had to be invented and built.

A still more important advance in the development of Western man's mind began with the introduction into Europe of machines for making paper and printing books. Invented by "infidel Arabs" these machines were first used, ironically, to print the Christian Bible. From 1456 onward, no more tedious hand copying, often illegible and full of errors; now clearly readable pages came sliding off the presses. At long last the sacred Book could be held in the hands of "the least of these." The sayings of Jesus could be read over and over again, sayings which priests did not always emphasize.

Of course in those early centuries the production and distribution of books was not as speedy as today, but even that slow stream of reading material wrought wonders for centuries to come. To learn, not just by hearsay, but by seeing the very own words of such thinkers as Roger Bacon and Thomas Aquinas brought about a new freedom, a new method of thought which far outstripped even the burgeoning in crafts. More priests could study and dare to quibble with the authority of Rome; Luther in Germany, Calvin in France, and Fox in England, demanded reform, a simpler, more spiritual religion, a religion closer to the New Testament, which they could now read.

And so it came about that man began to explore his own nature, his reasons for wanting certain things and not others; he compared what was, with what he thought ought to be. During the seventeenth and eighteenth centuries countless philosophical books were printed, translated and debated throughout Europe and Britain. The writings of Descartes, Locke and Voltaire, of Berkeley, Hume and Rousseau gave rise to endless disputations: God—pro and contra—matter and mind, morals, ethics, law and freedom. The Age of Inquiry, Reason and Enlightenment had burst into bloom. Endless probings pushed out against old boundaries seeking new ways of truth. Competition raged; reformation and revolution in church and state, in science and religion, left little room in the human heart for peace and worshipfulness.

Thus did Western man, in the fourteen centuries since 325 A.D., suffer the pains that attend growing from total dependence on one mammoth, inexorable, divinely ordained Authority into a daring and robust independence. *Homo sapiens* was growing into teen-age. Cocksure, he had cut loose from the inherited only to find that others, too, were willful, strong and often smart. He learned that it was not easy to change old assumptions and patterns of action. He found, too, that things were not exactly as he had been told and that he himself might have to change a little. During those centuries most men schemed for absolute power and self-aggrandizement. Yet there were some who could consider the whole situation, weigh benefits against harm. Like all adolescents man was subconsciously entangled with his juvenile experiences—nor did he know how far he still needed to go. The human species does not grow 'of a sudden,' all individuals at the same pace. But adolescence is one necessary step towards the maturing which alone can discern and try to co-ordinate the seething Mind forces which surround and indwell humanity.

Chapter Seven

DIVISIONS

The proliferation of books and the spread of education spawned new divisions in society. At first there had been the Church, the imperial military and the common people. Now the scholars and scientists gained status. Seeking explanation rather than self-aggrandizement, these men who had worked in isolation could now pool their findings, share their insights. After the Church of England withdrew from the Roman Church, Charles II of England even set up The Royal Society of London, a forum and center of publicity for scientists. Being able to read and utilize Galileo's and Newton's theories changed the world's notions of astronomy and gravity. Navigation became far less chancy. Physics, geology, chemistry and biology were wide open areas for probing. This new scientist class of persons explored and explained many things useful to the rest of their world.

Indeed, these scientists held secrets which were being gobbled up by still another division in society—the industrialists. In order to provide the ruling powers with their grandiosities and supply the demands of their practically continuous warrings and colonizings, there had to be enterprising underlings. The new materials and new processes thought up by scientists had to be produced, assembled and put to efficient use. The industrialists were the ones to do just that. They schemed out faster ways to convey coal and iron from underground; they constructed machinery for smelting and managed to roll out huge sheets of steel. These they used in place of wood for the hulls of ships. Installing steam engines instead of depending on wind in the sails made it possible to carry larger cargoes at much faster speeds. On long voyages to the Americas, southern Africa, Japan and Australia these new methods increased profits. Steam locomotives, too, could rush back with the wealth found in India. The industrialists were the ones who caused the eighteenth and nineteenth centuries to be known as the time of the Industrial Revolution which, to this day, has been gaining momentum.

Industrialism brought on another division in the social structure of those centuries. Gone was the artisan class, gone were the burghers who worked with personal dedication and creativity. The common man was more than ever at the mercy of the upper classes, first of the warring rulers and now of industry. The old partnership of craftsman and his beloved tools was scrapped—too slow, unreliable. "Manufacture" no longer meant *factura*, the making, by *manu*, hand. It suddenly meant standardized, immediately available, factory output. To the artisans it seemed as though their precious tools and instruments had conspired to quit the family workshop, convene in huge halls and blow themselves up into monsters. These monsters steamed and snarled and pounded away at them, battering their souls and squeezing the life out of their children.

The common people were burning with hostility not only against their employers but against the aristocracy as well. "Why all these warrings? Why have kings anyway?" Holland and Switzerland had long gotten on without kings. First thirty years of war, then seven years of war, all because the Grand Monarchs had ambitions. In Britain the kings had to obey the Parliament which had a House of Commons. In America the colonies had declared independence, had actually won, and no longer paid taxes to Britain. A few years later the common people of France broke out in rebellion—bloody rebellion. They guillotined the spendthrift royalty. Why should the crowned heads make war whenever they like and the common people either die or slave in factories?

For more than fifty years smouldering antagonism and rebellion among the commoners kept the crowned heads uneasy. Ethnic, religious and language factors aggravated the hostility. In 1821 the Christian Greeks rose up against Turkish overlordship. Not until 1829 could the combined forces of France, Britain and Russia give back to the ancient Greek democracy its independence. A German king was foisted upon it, however, to keep it docile. By 1830 revolts had erupted in Belgium, Italy, Germany and Poland. When these were quelled, parliaments were set up in France and Germany. They, too, were short-lived, and by 1852 the Grand Monarchs seemed once more to have the upper hand.

Once these democratizing attempts of the common people had been fended off, "the game of Great Powers was resumed with zest." In 1853 the Czar of Russia seized a time of clashes between Magyar Christians and the Moslem Turks to occupy the Danubian principalities. This, Britain and France agreed, must not be. The Danube, that long waterway to Persia and India, must not be in the hands of a country bigger than all the rest of Europe, immensely rich and in total control of its huge population. Russia had to be stopped, even if it took an alliance with Turkey to do it. By means of the Crimean War, ending in 1856, the Czar *was* repulsed.

Back in northern Europe nationalism was rife. In small wars boundaries shifted often and confusingly; Denmark, Italy and Austria lost territory to Prussia. No sooner had

Napoleon III of France let go of his overseas interests than he wanted a piece of the European pie and claimed Luxembourg. In 1870 Prussian forces invaded France; a year later Paris capitulated. The Treaty of Versailles left France a republic; Germany a united, all-German monarchy; Hungary and Austria a "Dual Kingdom." The map of Europe stayed roughly that way until the First World War.

But in the Balkans there was more trouble brewing—religious and political. Again the Christians claimed atrocities by the Turks, again Russia marched in. This time the Czar was the winner, and the Turks signed the Treaty of Stefano. But Britain did not relish the terms of that treaty—threatened war, and managed to draw up a new treaty according to which, except for a tiny spot at the Delta of the Danube into the Black Sea, Russia was ousted from Europe.

That 1878 Treaty of Berlin was only the last nineteenth century example of a series of multi-national conventions, councils and such, which began after Bonaparte's defeat at Waterloo. In 1818 the fashion started with what the crowned heads called "A Most Holy Alliance and Indivisible Trinity of Kings" and a "Concert of Europe." It purported to free the common man and protect true religion. These conventions were actually gala social events at which the lords and ladies displayed their power and riches. Usually they ended with a dividing of spoils in accordance with the whims of the cleverest sovereigns. Such attempts at peacekeeping persist as evidenced by the 1920 League of Nations and today's United Nations. These agreements, set up in solemn righteousness and seeming brotherhood, have as yet not succeeded in healing the divisiveness of late-adolescent humanity.

International warfare, fed by industrialism, kept Europe in turmoil throughout the nineteenth century. The common man's only solace was his private devoutness, his

faith in a caring God who would somehow, either in
heaven or hell, reward or punish with justice for all. Even
this sweet haven of inner peace was soon lost because of
the "Revolution against God" brought on by the scientists. Darwin's 1859 book *Origin of Species* set forth that
all animals, including man, evolve by natural selection,
not by the direct interference of God. Based on firsthand
observation Darwin and another naturalist had concluded
that, in the struggle for life, the unfit become extinct and
the more fit survive. The common man of the day, of
course, had neither the ability nor the time to read such an
erudite book. It might have gone practically unnoticed had
not three interested divisions of society pounced upon it
and declared their opinions of it.

The industrialists welcomed it because its subtitle—*Pres-
ervation of Favored Species*—encouraged them to be
strong, energetic, even as ruthless as Nature herself. The
'unfavored race' drudging away in factories would, sooner
or later, in any case, become extinct. Factory owners no
longer needed to feel guilty, confess to the priest or buy indulgences. Their commercial ambitions were furthermore
bolstered by Nietzsche's now popular cliché "God is
dead."

Next closest to the common man was his priest or minister. The theologians were enraged and fulminated against
the new theory with all the vigor they could muster. To say
that man was descended from the lowly ape was blas-
phemy; it negated the glorious story of six day creation
which is explicitly told in "God's Word." This outrageous
theory conflicted with the unshakable truth that Adam
was made in God's manlike image and that Eve was made
of Adam's rib. Worst of all, this heresy negated the doctrine of original sin and the need for man, the miserable
sinner, to do continual penance for his miserableness or
burn eternally in purgatory.

The third social division to spread the theory of evolution was that of the scientists. At a meeting of the prestigious Royal Society of London, biologist Thomas Huxley agreed that all species have evolved, and are still evolving, from simple to complex. Before that important assemblage he stated that he was not ashamed to have a monkey for an ancestor. A second scientist/philosopher/champion was Herbert Spencer who had himself written a book with the same theme entitled *The Development Hypothesis.* Scientists in general, proud of their new empirical method, labeled religion a silly belief in the supernatural, a sentimental superstition. All writings of the Age of Enlightenment were to them mere metaphysical quibblings to be scrapped. Natural laws and the world of physical matter were measurable, provable. Nothing else mattered.

During all that upheaval the commoner was dependent upon hearsay and the rantings of his preachers. From three sides he was being robbed of his last stronghold, his faith in a Savior crucified for man's sin and a heaven beyond the miseries on earth. If apes could become men, the poor factory slaves brooded, perhaps through industry and those monster machines, the poor could become rich and happy. There might even be more labor laws to free children from working twelve hours a day. Anyway, to rebel would cost them their livelihood; better stick with science and the new slogan "Science versus Religion."

Separateness was everywhere, not only between classes and levels of society but within the individual consciousness. Age-old motivations refuse to quit; they linger in the unconscious even while the rational mind says 'yes' to the new. Attempts at democracy had failed and yet a few labor laws were enacted. Change comes because of the clash between old patterns and new dreams and insights. Individual freedom had come to be one of man's dreams, strangely interwoven with old ideas of right and duty

Chapter Eight

RECONCILING THE DIVISIONS

As in each individual, so in the human species as a whole, maturing does not happen overnight. Even during the whole Darwin upheaval when separateness was climaxing, some signs of 'passage' into maturity appeared in the literate world. Some clear voices were heard tending to reconcile the divisions. Thinkers refused to deal only with a material world; religion was too deeply embedded in them to be thus coldly torn out and tossed aside. A few instances of their opinions on interconnectedness indicate the trend.

Darwin himself did not posit a crass division between his findings and the beloved Bible teachings. He did not deny the existence of a Most High. Nature lover that he was, he ended his epoch-making book with the statement that life had "been originally breathed by the creator into a few forms or into one . . . and from so simple a beginning endless forms most beautiful and wonderful have been evolved." Thomas Huxley neither denied nor affirmed the existence of God. Spencer, the other scientist champion of the theory of evolution wrote, "Let religion cease to picture the Absolute as a magnified man." Spencer reasoned that behind all appearances there is an Actuality, an original, unknowable homogeneous Force which, by slow modifications, differentiates Itself into the complexities of all matter and mind. He did not use the word God; for him "Actuality" was the core of truth in every religion.

Even while the slogan "Science versus Religion" was most clangorous, even while theologians were going insane because of the heretical theory of evolution, there were some thinkers open-minded enough, mature and compassionate enough, to reconcile the old with the new terminology. Henry Drummond, a Scottish clergyman who taught natural science on weekdays, was such a thinker. His mental attitude, he wrote in 1885, had been radically improved and enriched by the new discoveries in the natural world. He admitted that perhaps the theory "tampered with" theology, but had not Wycliffe, Luther, Henry the Eighth and others also 'tampered'? This scholar refused to shut his eyes to the fact that man's religious opinions are in flux; thereafter he let what he knew of natural science interflow with the flow of his religious opinions.

This theory of evolution, Drummond wrote, was unbiassed, unprejudiced, and uninfluenced by like or dislike. It was based on the unity and continuity of the natural universe. It gave to religion a base more solid than ecclesiastical authority. God the Unseen, the Spiritual World, was the origin of the natural world and its universal law. This theologian was willing to assume that natural law is the mode of operation, the process by which the Unseen, the Source and Cause, becomes visible. He agreed with Francis Bacon that science, more science, "wading deep into it, will bring men's minds to religion."

Unlike the "orthodox" religionists of all ages, and also unlike the cocksure Victorian scientists, Drummond argued against the sharp cleavage between matter and the spirit, against the notion of two-worlds-incommunicably-separate. Nature and the spirit, he was convinced, are indivisibly one; "the temporal is the husk and framework of the Eternal." To underline his idea he cited mining engineer Swedenborg: ". . . one would swear that the physical world was purely symbolical of the spiritual world." From Carlyle's *Sartor Resartus* he quoted, "Matter exists only to represent some idea, and body it forth."

Science textbooks have, of course, been updated many times since Newton's "final word" about matter and motion. The opinions of all the sciences have had to be in ever increasing flux as new experiments and better instruments have revealed cosmic forces never before known to exist. But religionists have seldom allowed their opinions to be in flux. Theologians still cling to their "text," descended from prehistoric Mesopotamian legends, a translation of countless previous translations. The "text," for them, still is the final and definitive "Word of God." If they, on their parts, could have admitted, perhaps at the turn of the century, that all scriptures are the insights of devout souls pondering the mysteries of life, if only they could have called them "Words ABOUT God," much of today's confusion, desolation and endangerment would not have occurred.

Emerson, another contemporary of both Darwin and Drummond, a trained theologian of mature humaneness, wrote, "The religion that is afraid of science dishonours God and commits suicide." Later this American transcendentalist declared, in his essay *Worship*, "There will be a new church, at first cold . . . the algebra and mathematics of ethical law . . . but it will have heaven (not the sky) and earth (not this planet only) for its beams and rafters, science for its symbol and illustration; it will fast enough gather beauty, music, picture and poetry. . . ." (parentheses added). But those few transcendentalists, viewers-of-the-world-as-one, could not break up the rigidities of institutional orthodoxy.

When science really began 'growing,' the scientists revised, "tampered with," their original pronouncements. They far outstripped the churchmen, even the transcendentalists, in understanding and interpreting the cosmos. What early science divided, mature science sees as unity; "wading deep," science is filling the gaps between matter, mind, emotion and law.

In 1928 Julian Huxley, grandson of the Darwin-championing Thomas Huxley, just about reversed the slogan "Science versus Religion." At a time when most scientists were highly skeptical of anything tinged with religion, this eminent biologist wrote a book titled *Religion Without Revelation* which had as its premise that a sense of the sacred, a religious emotion, always had, and always would exist in humankind. Almost thirty years after the original publication, there was sufficient demand for this book to warrant a revised and expanded edition. In two newly added chapters, he made it increasingly clear that the traditional doctrines, handed down from aeons past, needed now and again to be taken out for spring cleaning. The revised book demanded a developed religion, an evolved belief-system, a hypothesis befitting modern knowledge, scientific *and* spiritual. He gave it the name "Evolutionary Humanism."

For the emotion-packed word "God" Huxley favored a more abstract term, perhaps "Sacred Reality." He definitely felt the need of a new name for the Ultimate in his updated belief-system, a name without controversial connotations, a name with which the average anxious citizen can feel at ease. Unfortunately the word 'sacred' is, in this day of divorce, drug addiction and casual sex, out of fashion. Moreover, 'Sacred Reality' sounds complex, erudite and sanctimonious. The new name must be easy, contemporary, like a sport or a science one can 'get into.' Perhaps METAPHYSICS.

Now that compound nouns such as *cybernetics, electronics* and *astrophysics* have become household words, the term *metaphysics* seems appropriate. Though it was in disfavor with early science, today's generations are surely unaware of the scorn it evoked a century ago. Physics has been the obsession of technology; the prefix *meta,* meaning beyond, as in metabolism, metaphor and metatarsal, is not unfamiliar. Therefore the combining of *meta* with *physics* should no longer sound forbidding. The new name should offend neither the ardent believer nor the determined atheist; being nonreligious it is still not irreligious and certainly not anti-religious. It includes matter and what is beyond matter, the measurable and the im-mense, tangible and intangible, body and psyche. The Survival Team will welcome this noncommittal term.

What, in non-dictionary terms, *is* metaphysics? It is, quite simply, a concept of how the world works, of the architecture of the universe, physical and supraphysical. Philosopher Will Durant felt that "science assumes a meta-physic in its every thought." William James defined metaphysics as an "attempt to think things out clearly . . . to find their substantial essence in the scheme of reality." Alfred North Whitehead held that every archaic myth, every religion, every so-called cult is the metaphysical supposition of a given culture. "Apart from the metaphysical pre-supposition there can be no civilization." For today's Western civilization a new metaphysical concept must very soon become a firm working supposition.

In ages past man's wonder and religion gave rise to his science, his knowledge of the natural world; now it is the other way around: science proves that there is a Beyond. Cannot Huxley's 'sacred reality,' like Shapley's 'existence itself,' be merely a "spring-cleaned" phrasing of the time-honoured monosyllable God? Is it too much to expect this culture which invented the heat-seeking missile to accept the metaphysical supposition that what is seen, known and measureable emerges from an Unseen, Unknowable, All-transcending Beyond? Now that man has found the atom to be not one solid block of matter but rather a multiplicity of spinning members all participating in a dynamic togetherness, can he not be expected to theorize that *all* multiplicities of the known universe arise out of one still unanalyzable dynamism? Can he not assume, until the contrary is proven, that out of an *infinite* Isness, Omnipresence, Actuality, all *finite* clusters and combinations of clusters known as matter, become differentiated?

In making this metaphysical assumption and seeking to verify it man will need to consider its three aspects: the whole, its parts and their relatedness; in other words Infinitude, the Finite and the Great Law. As he finds the oneness, the inseparability of these three interdwelling phases of all that is, man will realize that he, standing midway between the atom and the galaxy, is in close partnership with all levels of the cosmic unity. Without dictates of priest and theology he will find intelligence, wonder and reverence. He need fear no distant Judge thundering at Job-like man; peace, compassion and fulfillment will dawn within his troubled soul. Man will think and feel in grander magnitudes. The entire cosmos will be his home, his law and his cathedral.

Chapter Nine

INFINITUDE

Metaphysics—the hypothesis that the cosmos is an all-inclusive unity—must begin with the study of that unity as Infinitude, the Totality, Source, Cause and Stuff of all being, the Whole, greater than the sum of Its parts. The most obvious feature of this unboundaried, un-ending, limitless Utmost is Its magnitude. Mathematicians have a symbol for It, a sort of figure eight lying on its side, whose outline leaves no opening. The layman accustomed to measuring definite units of space like inches or football fields or miles, is stumped by this symbol, to say nothing of astronomers' terms like a thousand million light years or their "googol," which denotes ten multiplied by itself a hundred times. As used in metaphysics the term Infinitude comprises the immensity of the cosmos; It pervades all of what seems like empty space, It comprises past and future time in Its eternal present, It enfolds and permeates all so-called solid matter from the minutest particle in the atom to the farthest-out supergalaxy.

More significant, however, than the bigness of the metaphysical Infinite, is the question of *what* It is. Humanity's guesses as to what It is constitute the history of every Myth, religion and philosophy as well as the most recent scientific theories of cosmology. Aeons ago man gave it names—Great Spirit, Brahman, Zeus, Ahuramazda, Yaweh, Allah, Lord or Father God. Names made It more visualizable, more like persons one could praise and beseech. Sometimes the names were too sacred to be spoken but always, when written, they were spelled with a capital letter. Though in metaphysics Its manlike character and beseechability are denied, Its Indispensability, Its Onlyness and Allness are emphasized. From earliest times deity has been given a capital initial; so this chapter will be replete with capitalized nouns and pronouns. And since this chapter attempts to convey the idea of an all-encompassing, all-pervading, pre-divinity, many names, totally impersonal nouns and pronouns, will replace traditional titles.

Perhaps the layman can borrow from astrophysics, the scientific discipline dealing with the vastness of space-time, in order to find appropriate terms. In that field 'space-time continuum' and 'undifferentiated pre-galactic material' are freely used. Moreover, astronomers are studying creation, past, present and future, what-is-and-how-it-came-to-be, the metaphysical supposition underlying Western man's existence.

In 1950 Fred Hoyle, known as the propounder of the theory of "Continuous Creation," wrote of a tenuous, diffuse and rarified general background which fills all space. He assumed that all celestial bodies, all the whirling, ever-expanding galaxies, are condensations of that tenuous, gaslike substance. The combined quantity of matter in the cosmos, he estimated, occupies less than a thousandth of the background tenuosity. In Hoyle's 1957 book, *Frontiers of Astronomy,* he enumerated several differing 'fields' in space, the outermost of which—the field beyond nuclear, electro-magnetic and gravitational fields—is called the *creation* field which causes matter to originate. That field dominates the largest aspects of the universe.

One gets the impression that by the interaction of energy

fields throughout the space-time continuum the rarified background becomes locally compressed into solar systems and clusters of systems all whirling within themselves and around each other at terrific speeds. These whirling bodies and all the 'material' within them become dense or diffuse as influenced by each other or by their various fields. To paraphrase this hypothesis for the layman who studies metaphysics: Infinitude, which is so diffuse and so rarified that it cannot be seen, condenses locally—that is, becomes differentiated—into solid forms, temporarily finite. As the pre-galactic material densifies into galaxies so does pre-finite Infinitude at times solidify into the finite.

The Steady State Cosmology is now rivalled by the "Big Bang Theory" which Jastrow, in a recent book called *God and the Universe,* claims has *no* competitors. The new claim is that the mass of all matter in the cosmos, trillions of degrees hot, suddenly exploded and sent what we know as galaxies hurtling out into space. This is thought to have happened twenty billion years ago; some astronomers claim still to be hearing vestiges of that bang. Eighty billion years hence a collapse is expected.

So big a blast might well have destroyed all evidence of what came before it. But must we not in common sense assume that there *was* a Somewhat which contained the ingredients of an explosion? Must there not have been an "Already-there-ness" which could explode? Could not the sudden violent blast have been merely the process by which the tenuous background, the "Hidden Stuff," the Primal Essence, condenses into matter, some of whose fragments constitute the Milky Way and its little planet earth?

Neither cosmology seems to deny that there has been, and still is, a vast unexplained space-time continuum, a Formlessness in which motion, light and form happen, in

which matter materializes and existence exists. Since man's
investigation of the ultra-small as well as of the ultra-large
both seem to be ending in mystery, Fred Hoyle felt it
might not be far-fetched to hope that the two mysteries
would turn out to be closely connected. In view of mankind's many guesses, scientific and religious, it does seem
'not very far-fetched' for the metaphysicist to suppose
that the two actually *are* one mystery. Does it not seem
reasonable that within one infinite, homogeneous, fluidic
Essence, densities can occur in varying degrees of solidness
and porosity?

Matter is the "appearance" by which we are warned not
to judge. Matter is fenced off, finite, having edges and
endings of a sort: gravity, magnetism, electricity and the
gamut of chemicals, flaming stars, water and wind, the
planets and their myriad populations. And yet finite matter is in continuous process of change; though structured,
it is in flux, stimulates other matter, responds, has rhy-
thms and patterns in its combinings and dissolvings. Cush-
ioned in Infinitude's dynamism, the finite appears and dis-
appears, emerges, evolves, melts back and re-emerges.

Could it be that Hoyle's 'Rarified General Background'
and Shapley's 'Existence Itself,' being synonyms for Infinitude, merit being spelled with a capital initial? The Bible parable reads: "And God said, Let the waters . . . be
gathered together unto one place, and let the dry land appear: . . . And God called the dry land earth . . . " (Gen:
1:9, 10) "Waters gathered together" is more poetically
phrased than the astronomers' statements, but synonym
and parable do seem to express the same idea.

Modern quantum physicists come even closer to metaphysics than the astronomers in that they now recognize
the porosity of the seemingly solid finite to the tenuous,
rarified and subtle aspects of Infinitude. They recognize
the indwellingness of mindlike, perceptive and cognizant

qualities in "solid" matter. Eminent researcher Fritjof Capra, for instance, in his 1975 book *The Tao of Physics,* parallels the perceptions of ancient mystics with the findings now being arrived at by means of sophisticated technological instruments. More than 2,500 years ago, before a telescope was ever invented, the Hindu, Buddhist and Taoist mystics knew by intuition—taught from within— that spirit and matter are one organic whole. They sensed, without equations or computers, that the universe is one "unbroken wholeness" in which "all things are interdependent and inseparable parts . . . of the same cosmic reality." "Cosmic breath" was often used to describe Infinitude.

Interspersing ancient mystical writings with diagrams and equations which express the conclusions of 'the new physics,' Capra indicates that to the observing, experiencing mind, the universe is "a dynamic, inseparable whole which always includes the observer in an essential way." "In atomic physics the scientist cannot play the role of a detached observer, but becomes involved in the world he observes to the extent that he influences the properties of the observed objects." Capra quotes from another physicist who wrote, "One has to cross out that old word 'observer' and put in its place the new word 'participator.' In some strange sense the universe is a participatory universe." As did the ancients, modern atomic scientists assume that "the universal interwovenness includes the human observer and his or her consciousness."

That word 'consciousness'—knowing-with-ness—is an important word in the study of metaphysics. Who knows how much consciousness the oceans have, or Half Dome in Yosemite or a willow tree? We do know that the human species has consciousness; we do know that consciousness, during its short span in evolution, has been absorbing ever larger amounts of imagination, awareness and mental acuity. Since Infinitude is the one Source and Stuff, *mind, mental activity* must be among Its attributes. "The entire cosmos, in all its vastness," Julian Huxley stated, "consists of the same world stuff . . . is not restricted to material properties . . . is capable of eliciting mental activity." As far back as 1929 Arthur Eddington, Professor of Astronomy at the University of Cambridge, England, delivered the annual lecture of the Society of Friends under the title *Science and the Unseen World.* One would expect so eminent an astronomer to be most concerned with the world that can be *seen.* In later years he made the much quoted statement, "The stuff of the world is mind stuff."

These quotations from the hard sciences are not intended as proof, merely as parallels to the metaphysical hypothesis that an immaterial Actuality becomes locally differentiated as a material, measurable finite. Does not the diffuse vapor in a cloud sometimes form raindrops or snowflakes or hailstones? Magnify hailstones into galaxies and minify rain into atoms. In metaphysical language Infinite Mind is the Omnipresent. Nothing can be added to It and nothing can be excluded from It. It is the Beyond-and-Within of all that ever was, now is, and ever will be. Without diminishing Itself Infinitude condenses various assortments of Its myriad properties into *subsidiary phases of Itself*—the finite universe.

Thus far, the immensity, the tenuousness and the compressibility of the Cosmic Matrix have been considered. Now Its two most significant, most awe-inspiring attributes must come into focus: Omnipotence and Omniscience—aliveness and intelligence.

ALIVENESS

If what the ancient mystics sensed and the quantum physicists are confirming is the best approximation so far possible of how the universe works, the metaphysicist is not too far off. If, as they assume, the cosmos is an indivisible Whole, then all components of It must be available throughout Its entirety. No one will deny that aliveness happens but as yet it can be reliably detected only when encased, incarnated, bodied forth, in some see-able subsidiary phase of the Unseen. Even when it can be observed, one cannot observe what it is, only what it *does,* how it behaves, *in* and *as* the creation it inhabits. Its tenancy in a given structure varies, thirty days in a fruit fly, six hundred years in the Sequoia. Observable or not, "Life did not literally begin. Life is. Life is everywhere everywhen. . . ."

No longer does one divide the world into separate "kingdoms," inanimate or animate, mineral, vegetable or animal; in every ray of light, every drop of water and grain of sand there is aliveness. Without it no buttercup or bumble bee, no dove or dolphin, no Abraham, Plato or Jesus. At appropriate intervals life activity seems to withdraw from one phase into new combinations with other ingredients of Infinitude, distributing itself in new patterns and tempos, or "relaxing" as pure abstract Essence. There is no death; aliveness does not cease, it eternally intermeshes with other aspects of the One Mystery. Writes aviator-philosopher Guy Murchie, "Along with moons, planets . . . stars, galaxies . . . the Universe itself is a growing, metabolizing supersuper Being, in very truth alive."

INTELLIGENCE

No one in this age of research and technology can belittle the intelligence displayed by some human beings. Staggering as that is, the intelligence of Infinite Mind exceeds it a zillionfold. Man has only recently gained an inkling of the wisdom which structures the lowliest beastie, provides for birthing, feeding, mating and so dying that others may live. The intelligence factor of Infinite Mind designs, builds, operates and maintains the makings of every atom, the leaf of every tree, the eye, the mind and flight of every bird and the circling of every star-sprinkled galaxy. It inflows each finite thing and every combination of things. It has been so efficient that some species have needed no change for countless aeons. And yet, if other factors demand change, Ominscience shows astonishing ingenuity in producing adaptation, mutation, evolution or extinction: sea creatures become amphibious, tree dwellers walk the ground.

As a rule only the botanist will seriously "consider the lilies of the field," the dandelion and the oak, but if the layman will bother to look, he too will marvel at the whiter-than-alabaster calla emerging from its brownish bulb; he, too, will wonder at the infinitesimal helicopters sent out to make next year's crop of lawn stars and at the acorn which knows how to become a fifty foot tree. Most amazing and mysterious of all, Omniscience indwelling the human frame has taught man to see, hear, remember, hope for, invent and build instruments with which to achieve such miracles as brain surgery and the corneal transplant.

Chapter Ten

THE FINITE WORLD

The finite world is the aggregate of all matter, all 'subsidiary phases' of Non-matter considered in the chapter just ended. It is the world of solid material which floats in the Immaterial "as the earth floats in the soft arms of the atmosphere." It is the realm of density and structure, of all created things from seaweed to sequoia, from plankton to porpoise to primate and of every submicroscopic constituent of any and all of these. The finite world is the sum total of all differentiations, condensations and compactions of Infinitude. Before quantum physics evolved the finite world was thought to be much like a huge machine made of tiny but solid building blocks called atoms. The average layman still does not realize what researchers in the New Physics have discovered, namely, that the universe is not a machine but an organism with all parts delicately attuned to each other and to the Environment.

As previously stated, gods there always were: all-powerful, Magicians by whatever name; they had to be kept friendly by rituals and ceremonials as specified by the priesthood. At first the gods were expected to arrange man's finite world. But as living became more complicated, man himself did more and more in the way of managing his daily world. The neolithic planter, for instance, still held his rain dance and seasonal rituals but when it came to his ordinary chores he began using his own cleverness. Weary of pushing his plowstick through sun-dried soil he thought up a trick by which he could harness his ox and make him do the work. In Mesopotamia, once the priests' ceremonial demands had been met, the laymen took personal charge of farming and trading strategies.

So it came about that little by little, as priestcraft developed, dogma and worship activities were set apart from routine pursuits, the one holy, divine, and the other temporal, "of the flesh." Man, having long since confessed that he was a miserable sinner, accepted the additional guilt for dabbling in the carnal, finite world. And yet, in matters of his intimate territory, home, food and family, he knew that he himself had to do whatever improving he desired. He proceeded diligently on the basis that things and persons were distinct, separate objects to be handled with almost mechanical skill—often with force—or else destroyed. This inherited sense of sin, this sense of two separate, even opposing worlds, lingers in the subconscious of today's man, even in the unconscious of those who have long since dropped all religion or religious sentiment out of their conscious reckonings. The notion of duality, of dichotomy, is the *mistake,* the missed target, mistranslated as *sin* by the professional priesthood.

It must be the goal of the new metaphysic to explain away all ideas of separateness, of things locked in form. What science has proven must now be assimilated and metabolized in lay consciousness: the finite world is the tangible 'offspring' of the intangible World Stuff—"without form and void." (Gen. 1:2) It is the many born of the One; it is an incarnation of parts of the discarnate Already-there-ness. As an analogy, take a large family born of the same parents. No two children display the same characteristics and yet, somewhere in their ancestry all their various traits did exist. As generations go by, these children become the ancestors of still more body-and-character-components.

To each generation its forbears are less tangible, more hidden, abstract. The earliest ancestor, however, indwells all. What each child does with the inherited equipment becomes that child's destiny, his expanded or diminished finite achievement. This concept, raised to the nth power, may suggest the way by which the finite world inherits and utilizes the potentials of the Prefinite.

Could it be that this concept was what the Man of Galilee intended to convey when he said to his disciples, "Call no man your father upon the earth: for one is your Father, which is in heaven"? (Matt. 23:9) The early Christians, and consequently most Christian sects of today, did not understand him. They considered Jesus to be the "only begotten Son of God," the *only* incarnation of the Almighty, whereas Jesus knew that not only he himself but all others also were sons of the Father, incarnations of the One. He knew that the grass of the field, the fowl of the air, the vine and the husbandman, the traveler, the thief, the Samaritan, even the adulteress—all are *in* the finite world but not *of* this world; all are born, rather, of the Transcendent One. Like the earlier mystics, Jesus knew it and gave his life to teach it. For the men of his time the idea was too abstract; even his ardent followers had to compromise with the primitive concrete image of God, unreachably far off, issuing orders like a Roman caesar, angry and vengeful, punishing or playing favorites.

Not by the commands of a cosmic autocrat, but by each entity's use or non-use of its inherited endowment, does any finite entity prosper, evolve, or succumb to its surroundings. Each individual and each community of creatures de-term-ines its uniqueness, growth and usefulness. By its own efforts are its 'terms' and limits either expanded or shrunken. Once formed, all that is finite, *all* from minnows to man to mountain ranges, is involved with all else, finite or infinite. The very limits are the challenges which make body battle against body, mind against mind, individual against community. On all levels the world of form is the arena for testing, refining and redefining differentiated bodies and the Mind aspects individualized within them.

It seems clear that the human species excels most other species in being the carrier of an exceptionally large proportion of the mind potentials of Infinitude. Despite man's very recent arrival on the planet—compared, for instance, with the amoeba—he has managed to gather, store, organize and pinpoint his consciousness upon discovering how the finite world functions. He has puzzled, compared and extrapolated. It seems as though, by putting to use his individualized mind he invites appropriate Mind Stuff to flow in. Asking of himself, he receives from the All; seeking within himself, he finds the One. Then he can knock upon the closed door, and it will open to him. By channeling the Inflow he has, through the centuries, discerned certain physical laws describing the processes of the natural world. The sciences are rife with results of the "asking, seeking and knocking" of individuals such as Newton, Ohm and Einstein.

These natural laws, unlike the laws of Moses or the Church or the State, are not man-made; they are merely man-discerned, man-deduced. They are self-implementing, self-enforcing and they cannot be abrogated. They are merely the modes of operation found to prevail in finitude. Only when man has precisely complied with them does his proposed finite action succeed. The slightest miscalculation can blow up a space rocket and incinerate the astronauts inside it. Failing to obey these physical laws, operative since the earth cooled, man becomes the victim of his own mistakes.

With wits so sharpened as to bring about unprecedented

creature comforts, laser and quartz technology, man is still desperately unhappy. He has houses, cars, cameras and telephones, and yet, having cut himself adrift from Infinitude, he feels disconnected. Hungry for deep value, he settles for junk food, the sensations of sex, drugs and crime.

Though man has "waded deep into science," as Bacon advised, he has not waded deeply enough to discern that there is a law that goes beyond the known laws of matter, a process, a *modus operandi* which supersedes all natural laws. This law concerns the Mind factor of the finite world which only a few imaginative seekers have thus far partially discerned and formulated.

Chapter Eleven

THE LAW OF MIND

The third aspect of this triune metaphysic concerns most specifically the inter-relatedness of the finite world within itself and the finite-Infinite commingling. Scientists have discerned numerous natural laws—the processes involved as differentiations interact with one another. Sometimes, of course, more than one natural law is in operation. That the diverse laws co-ordinate is taken into account. Is the reason for such co-ordination a matter of chance or of physics or of some Law of laws that has not yet been discerned? If the seen, finite universe arises in an infinite Unseen universe, could it not be that there is a similar continuity linking the many physical laws to one *pre-physical* Overlaw? As there is one continuity of *Substance,* so there is one continuity of *process*—one Great Law of laws in which the calculations about gravity and electricity are merely the local outworkings. The metaphysic here being considered makes this assumption and, since the World Stuff is Mind Stuff, names the Overlaw the *Law of Mind.*

When the Law of Mind is clearly known and intelligently applied, it will be more significant and rewarding for modern humanity than the discovery of the Americas and the industrial revolution were to Central Europe. How it was first perceived and applied will be outlined in later chapters. What it is, what it does and how it pertains to man's life, liberty and pursuit of happiness must first be clarified.

Since finite mind is actually Infinite Mind in visibility, no created thing, no be-ing, no event or process is without some degree of Mind activity. Indwelling the forms through which It is differentiated from Its own Allness, Mind proceeds in Its orderly ways to fulfill the demands of Its creation. "Be ye therefore perfect, even as your Father which is in heaven is perfect." (Matt. 5:48) The *quality* and *intensity* of mind action in each and every finite form—in rocks, ocean waves, light or sound waves, in grass and trees and turtles and man—are disseminated throughout the universe, both seen and Unseen. The dissemination takes place in ways as ordered and reliable as the workings of a fine motor car. Any vehicle performs in accordance with the nature of its engine and the fuel activating it. The engineers know the physical laws involved in both mechanism and fuel. Without individual mind to turn on ignition—make the connection—so that Mind Fuel may flow, the finite form does not function, grow, evolve or coordinate. The One Great Law, with the help of its errand-boy natural law, *processes* the qualities and intensities of mind activity into form and event.

The processing is accomplished not by leaping from mind to Mind and back, but by *soaking through,* by a subtle sort of osmosis, as by adding a dye to a clear solution so that any fabric dipped into it will take on the dye color. Of course the Law of Mind has to deal with many diverse qualities of many diverse intensities, all interpenetrating. To use a minor human example: Sally yearns for glory. As a teenager she is exuberantly confident and seems to be 'making it'; her dating and early marriage are glamorous; her baby Jane is adorable. But as a mother, Sally

finds life rather dull, feels neglected and becomes dis-
gruntled. What she thinks and says and does in her peev-
ish dissatisfaction soaks through into Infinite Mind—
soaks into the Solution in which the entire finite world is
floating, seeps into all individual minds, altering, modifying, infecting them. The greed quality and reactions to it
bounce back and forth within Sally's family and circle of
friends. All situations are tempered, or intensified or radically changed because the Law of Mind, responding to
Sally's unhappy and unloving thoughts, spreads the pollution into all other finite minds, near and far as man meas-
ures. The Law of Mind knows no distance, only order.

The intelligence of Infinitude indwells every finite creation and surrounds all individual minds. When invited, It
gives even more, and more specifically, of Itself. What the
individual does with his ration of Mind Stuff, whatever he
desires, intends, or demands consciously or subliminally,
steers the Law of Mind in the stipulated direction. That
Law is never not in operation; a change in mind quality
and intensity merely deflects the law's course or speeds, or
slows it. There is no stopping it. Mind is the substance, the
Law is the process. What mind intends the Law brings
about, whether the "intender" is a hen or a human. Like
all physical laws this Law is neutral; it does not judge,
praise or punish; it just *is*. Whether the intention results in
good or in harm depends solely on the initiating mind
waves. Man is the chooser; the Law is the doer.

Mind waves emanate, like auras, from every finite body,
interblending with other auras to modify the mental cli-
mate. Wild animals sense these mind waves, pets know
their owners' moods and intentions, plants respond by
thriving or withering; can it be that the human unconscious is less sensitive? The wave lengths of fear, anger,
greed, malice and violence are stress-producing. They
cause static, interference, blockages. On the other hand,

peace, kindness, confidence seep in, like sunshine, and dissolve resistances. Whether hostile or compassionate, every entity gives off wave lengths which penetrate the minds of all other mind-entities surrounding it. Each individual mind is, like a civilian band radio, both a sender and a receiver. Each must adjust his mental antenna and tune in to the wave lengths it desires.

Like the equations describing the laws of physics, the Law of Mind has an equal sign in the middle. If one side of an equation changes, the other side must also be adjusted. Balancing the two sides of the equal sign is achieved by the Law of Mind. The Law orchestrates, synchronizes, choreographs all mind waves—finite and Transfinite—to make manifest the sum total of what has been thought into it. That every thought, every dream, every unconscious motive sets off chain reactions confronting other chain reactions throughout the universe, is accomplished by the Law of Mind. This truth, currently being explored and formulated, must now come to be the basic assumption, the fundamental premise, of every rational being.

Chapter Twelve

FINDING THAT MIND MATTERS

Terms concerning matters of mind were coined in the golden age of Greece—terms like *psyche* and *soma* or *physis, noumenon* and *phenomenon, sophia*—meaning wisdom—and *philosophia*—meaning love of wisdom. In those days it was generally accepted that the god of healing sidetracked the waking mind and did his cures while patients were asleep. But these methods fell into disuse in the five centuries of warring under Alexander, the great Greek, the Persians and then the Romans. The Man of Galilee made the blind to see and the lame to walk merely by being in their presence, by telling them to believe they were or would be healed. But, said the organized Christian Church, only Jesus could do that because he was the Son of God. Thus it was that throughout the Middle Ages and into the Age of Reason, the treatment of disease depended on bloodletting (leeching), on a few herbal remedies or else on amateur surgery.

Even as late as the American Revolution when the laws of mechanics were zealously applied in industry it had surely never been dreamed of that there might be a Law of Mind. If miraculous things happened without physical power or tools, they were thought to be by direct intervention of God through means of some priest or saint who had a favored place in the Kingdom. And yet, in those days before anaesthesia a Viennese surgeon, without invoking divine intervention, induced unawareness of pain and healing in his patients. Unwittingly he was, in the 1700's, applying the Law of Mind.

That surgeon, Anton Mesmer, noticed that when he placed his scalpel or some other metallic object on the afflicted area the patient fell into a sleep and, upon awaking, was healed. Soon he discovered that he could get results without any 'magnetic object,' merely by standing next to the patient. He then called the force "animal magnetism." News of such miraculous doings spread fast. Mozart recommended to him a young pianist, protegée of the Empress of Austria. After some time of working with Mesmer, this lady, blind from early childhood, received her sight and became a prominent composer and court concertist. When Mesmer later worked in Paris, his fellow professionals were outraged. They appointed a royal commission to investigate such unorthodox procedure. The verdict was that the cures were all based on imagination. Dr. Mesmer retired to a small Swiss village and avoided the limelight. He must have continued in his special way, however, for in the year 1838 a student of his toured New England giving lectures and demonstrations of Mesmerism.

At one of those lectures in Belfast, Maine, a local clockmaker named Phineas Parkhurst Quimby was captivated by the new idea. Determined to find out how such a thing could be, he began experimenting with anyone who would consent to be his subject. After a few years he found an excellent and willing subject, a highly sensitive clairvoyant known as Lucius. When mesmerized this young man placed his hands on Quimby's lower back which had for years been very painful. He stated that the afflicted parts would heal. Next day the pain was gone, a thing the doctors had claimed impossible. Years later Quimby wrote that he had, since that day, never experienced the pain.

For four years Quimby and Lucius traveled about together, often assisting doctors in making diagnoses, sometimes giving public performances. The demonstrations were as follows: Quimby put Lucius into trance and awaited his diagnosis of the case. The silent clockmaker then telepathically gave instructions to be voiced by Lucius to patient and audience.

In 1847 Quimby ceased making public appearances which he later called "mesmeric humbuggery." For the next twelve years he worked alone, "sitting with" his patients in his office, even travelling to their homes or answering their letters. His procedure was first to determine the patient's "erroneous opinion" about his ailment and then to concentrate his own thought so intensely on wholeness of mind and body as to build a similar belief in the patient.

Since most of his patients had been given up as incurable by medical doctors, "Dr. Q's" healings were gratefully and enthusiastically talked about. Though in puritanical New England such things might well have been labeled witchcraft, this man's honesty and friendly concern won him ever increasing devotion. By 1856 he was working for and with some five hundred patients a year. During that time he tested and modified his theories and became convinced that the cures happened because he was using the same principle that Jesus used. He therefore called his method "Truth" or "Science of Health," even "Christ Science." By this time he had concluded that it was not his own intelligence but rather that, during consultation, his own and his patient's minds were opened to the great, non-personal Life Force. Since he did not freely use the word "God" he spoke of that Force as "Divine Wisdom."

By concentrating on "the inner Spirit which never sins and is never sick," he dispelled from his own mind and that of his patients their life-disturbing opinions. For Quimby it was not a matter of magnetism or mesmerism, nor even of mind-to-mind telepathy; it was a matter of individual mind being open to Divine Mind.

In 1859 his following had grown so large that Quimby moved his office to Portland where he could have his son's help in keeping records. Son George was the only one in the office who had not had a spiritual mind healing. The Misses Ware kept every word of their beloved "Dr. Q's" writings, preserved all drafts of essays he intended some day to publish and made several sets of "Fifteen Questions and Answers" which could be lent to "deserving" patients. Julius Dresser, healed in 1860 of typhoid pneumonia, devoted much time to conversing with new patients and joining in post-treatment discussions. From 1862 on Mrs. Patterson, healed after years of invalidism, frequented the office and eagerly sought to know details of Quimby's method. She borrowed "Fifteen Questions" from Dresser. Several times she lectured and wrote articles for local newspapers describing Quimby's remarkable cures. The office was so busy and the demands on "Dr. Quimby" so severe that in 1866 his strength gave out. All office records were most carefully guarded; for many years no one could pry the originals out of son George's possession.

But those who had been healed were impatient and went out, like the twelve disciples of old, to spread the good news. In 1869 a Swedenborgian minister named Evans published *Mental Cure* which put into more erudite words the New England clockmaker's simple writings. In 1870 Mrs. Patterson, now the world-known Mary Baker Eddy, published her *Science of Man,* giving full credit to Quimby, her "sage profound"; but in 1872, having waited six years after his death, she made no more mention of Quimby. In successive editions of her *Science and Health* she replaced more and more of his ideas with her own. Because Mrs. Eddy organized classes wherever she happened to be, her work did much to spread interest in and concern with matters of mind.

Other recovered patients, lacking the ability to write and publish books, kept Quimby's ideas alive by founding "Truth Centers" and "New Thought Groups" in their home towns. Original manuscripts being unavailable, these groups were also based on personal interpretations. Meantime writings by Whitman, Thoreau and Emerson were fostering religious sentiment. A great wave of liberal Christianity swept across the country. Any and all of numerous controversies as to the originator of spiritual mind healing have added publicity and popularity to the movement. Today hundreds of thousands of persons believe that matters of mind are of great importance in man's health and affairs.

In Europe, during this same third of the century, not Transcendentalism but Darwinism was gripping hundreds of thousands by insisting that only matter was of importance. Granted, mind was useful for discovering and applying the laws of nature—gravity, magnetism and electricity —but in all other ways mind was *im-material,* incorporeal, and therefore of no consequence. Physics mattered: metaphysics was nonsense. Due to this surge in materialism European culture changed: city life brought in new social freedoms, new sexual vogues; parents and children lost common values. Significantly larger numbers of what seemed to be cases of hysteria confronted the medical profession. Again, some fifty years after Quimby heard about Mesmer, someone came upon the idea that mind might be the cause of the trouble.

This someone was, of course, Sigmund Freud. As is now well known, Freud concluded, after listening to the dreams his patients described, that their neuroses were caused by desires unfulfilled and therefore repressed. This unique idea presupposed that mind, consciousness, consists of levels not recognized during waking hours, consists of levels deeper than the rationalizing intellect. Freud's first book, *Interpretation of Dreams*, and his founding of the "International Psychoanalytic Association" caught the attention of other neurologists. Adler, Jung and Rank joined this movement which considered mind worthy of scientific investigation. All of these, in their maturer writings developed their own, somewhat divergent theories as to man's yearnings and motivations.

Due to the insights of these four early twentieth century thinkers psychology and psychiatry have become highly respected sciences dealing with the layerlike nature of the human mind and its bearing upon the body and behavior of the personality. The terms *subconscious, unconscious, preconscious,* even *psychoid,* have come into common parlance. Countless pseudosciences have come into vogue: communal bathing in warm pools, pillow punching, human potential seminars, primal scream techniques. These attempts at improving consciousness are listed not to pass judgement on them, but rather to point out that the plethora of such enterprises and the multitude of persons taking part in them, stand as proof positive that the state of man's mind does indeed make a considerable difference in his personal and social well-being. Not only advanced quantum physicists like Capra, but the foremost scientists of medicine, biology and psychology have at last discovered that MIND MATTERS. Mind is Source, process *and* product. Mind is what matters most of all.

Now that the human species is so perilously close to the point of mental, moral and physical self-destruction, can we hope that, in the Survival Team's improved environment, the Toms and Sallys of the coming decades will be open to the new metaphysic and accept the fact that mind *matters*—that mind is the universal dynamism by which the finite world evolves? The very expectation by those who read these pages will set the course of the Great Law. Let each reader resolve and expect that laymen as well as scientists will find a clearer, more plausible world perspective. It must be obvious, self-understood, that not physical force but the thoughts, the desires and purposes of individual minds shape the future of all the finite world. Man is the chooser and must learn to choose qualities and intensities of mind which will, through the action of the Law of Mind, bring about for this planet's populations well-being and creative wisdom.

PART TWO

Chapter One

MAN THE CHOOSER

All chapters thus far have set forth the deplorable state of today's society and the urgent need for a more mature understanding of man's place in his inner and outer world. Eminent thinkers have been quoted to indicate how threatening conditions are, why they are so threatening and what must be done if man is to survive. The author has stated the opinion that modern man's sense of uprootedness is the cause of his desperation. She has set forth a metaphysical world view which, she is convinced, will foster a renewed sense of partnership in human evolution. All this she has outlined in an impersonal way, almost as an instruction manual might describe the use of a new air conditioner.

Beginning with this chapter, however, the author wishes no longer to serve as an observer making objective statements. She now wishes to join with any and all who have read to this point as a co-worker in exploring and practicing the new metaphysic. Sentences will henceforth be phrased more subjectively—not "mankind is," "the individual can" and "there is no separateness," but rather "*we all* are made of the One Mind" and "I am my own keeper and my brother's brother."

Let us not think that the new metaphysic is a profana-
tion of the beloved Judeo-Christian Story. Far from it.
Not a rejection, not a denunciation, only a desire to see its
full, deep meaning with greater perspective. Knowing that
all religions are hallowed collections of lore and legend, we
must reinterpret them, much as an adult reinterprets the
fables he heard in childhood. We must sense expanded
meanings, recognize verities once beyond our ken. In order to keep pace with scientific advances we must see all
theologies as venerable landmarks along man's pathway to
maturity. We must read the ancient scriptures as parables,
attempts to convey mystical meanings without adequate
language.

The early Christian churches were scattered among
alien people of diverse ethnic backgrounds, all herded
together under Greco-Roman overlordship. The apostles
who worked at far distances from one another had to be
very positive about the new doctrine. There could be no
equivocal points; what each one decreed was ortho-dox,
meaning *the right, true doctrine,* according to the first
hand information of the founding apostle. The office of
church father or priest was held by every succeeding priest
by divine right of apostleship. Once more there was
authority; once more there was a sharp line between
'truth' and heresy. Around the periphery heathen practices did creep in, prompted surely by the need somehow
to let the new show elements of the old and familiar.

Thus it happened, too, that the Asiatics took kindly
to the Trinity, a holy family in which they felt protected,
Father, Son and Holy Ghost. These were imageable, useful. But with as much hindsight as we now have can we
not see in the Trinity a foreshadowing of the new metaphysic—the Infinite begetting the finite? Then the Holy
Ghost can be seen as an ineffable interflowing, the Law of

Mind connecting the All with all, self-enforcing, inviolable. Science uses the terms essence, process and product. Are they not a parallel tri-unity?

Once we recognize this parallel between the ancient stories, science and metaphysics, we can begin applying the Law of Mind intelligently, with intent to harmonize and placate the conflicting layers of our consciousness. We must study, re-survey our inherited drives, evaluate them in the light of *today's* values and think ourselves into quietness, understanding and participation. Only thus can we perceive what our particular, private, long term yearnings are, what values would fulfill the self we have thus far made of ourselves. Those yearnings we must choose as goals. Choose we must, for it is *our* mental and emotional choice which steers the Law of Mind. An unchoosing quality of mind produces nondescript experience. Muddled thinking—wishing or limply hoping—manifests as muddled experience. A mind that merely drifts causes us to drift among circumstances (things standing around) caused by more specifically thinking minds.

Adam, Abram, Moses and Jesus made choices. Constantine, Columbus, Freud, Edison and Lindbergh made choices that transformed their civilizations. Each chooser had to bear the consequences of the choice he made. The Law of Mind, the orderly process, responded to the thought currents of these choosers on a scale far grander than they envisioned. Finite choices affect not only the immediate surroundings; they expand old limits and alter intricate balances in accordance with each new choice. The mind energies of Infinitude recombine in new patterns. Thus evolution or endangerment.

Setting a goal is, of course, what activates both the individual mind and the Great Law. But there is more to it than that. The ways by which the goal is to be reached must not be fraught with adverse motivations. Impatience, greed, envy or vengeance trigger the Law to produce negatives for ourselves as well as for those against whom we have directed them. Malevolent emotions manifest as conflicts, stumbling blocks, delays, even failure. In Proverbs 10:12 (circa 450 B.C.) it is written, "Hatred stirreth up strifes. . . ." Circa 1950 A.D. humanist Abraham Maslow wrote, "Love actualizes, non-love stultifies." When delays and conflicts arise, we must check our own attitudes, not blame circumstances or other persons. To counteract inertia and contrariness of environment, individual or cultural, requires of us clear, tolerant understanding and persistent right choosing.

Let us take another mundane analogy to explain why, in matters of mind as well as mechanics, we must be circumspect about making choices. An automotive engineer plans a long journey. First of all he sees to it that he has ample fuel and that the fuel line is open. Then he checks all individual mechanisms in the engine and makes sure that each one is properly co-ordinated with every other mechanism. Connections must be secure; mixing, timing, thrusting and cooling must be ad-justed, ac-commodated. There must be no obstruction, no friction. The motor must run smooth and sweet. The prefixes *ad* and *co,* as in adjust and accommodate, when used in making choices, signify relatedness, co-operation, caring, 'other-regardingness' in mind journeys as well. The finite individual must be un-blocked in order to allow Infinite Mind Fuel to flow in Its orderly way and deliver peak performance. If we can apply the Great Law caringly, benevolently, there will be few stallings.

This, too, the ancient prophets knew. Trouble is, we do not bother to appreciate Biblical language. The first Commandment, of course, was "to love the Lord your God," (substitute Infinite Mind) "to walk in all his ways . . . " and next, "love ye therefore the stranger, for ye were strangers in Egypt." (Deut. 10:19) In Leviticus 19:18 we read, "Thou shalt not avenge nor bear any grudge. . . , but thou shalt love thy neighbor as thyself." In the ancient Aramaic language, the word 'love' had to cover the gamut of feelings from adoration to honesty to kindliness. The prophets of those days did not know there was a Law of Mind, an infallible, uninterruptible Orderliness, but they *did* know that love matters. Now that we, neither prophets nor scientists, know that there is such a Law, that love is a matter of mind and that mind matters most of all, let us learn to use love and mind and Law intelligently.

Intelligent use of the Law of Mind implies guarding all our choices against overintensity. Certainly we must love, but just as certainly our love must not be overindulgent. There must, in matters of loving and rejecting, be calmness, balance and logical evaluation. Our choices and decisions must be made with an open-minded willingness to allow for unknown factors. Our own unconscious drives and the inherited thought patterns of others all influence the course of the Law. As Julian Huxley put it, we must rise to a "new level of co-operative interthinking."

Now that we have a certain knowingness about the way the Law works we must remember that we always deal, not with matter, but with *pre-matter,* with qualities and intensities of mind which are to be manifested. Only by wise use of the Law of Mind can we expand, perfect and even transcend ourselves. We must always, undeviatingly, keep aware of the interpenetration of Mind and Law with finite mind, matter and events. Only thus can we make choices that are wholesome, unifying and symbiotic. As persons seeking to be self-perfecting, and indeed as "agents of evolution," we must knit together the ways of scientist, layman, poet and mystic.

Chapter Two

MIND TECHNIQUE

We who know that the Law of Mind responds to the slightest mental charge have a special way of keeping our thoughts compatible with the metaphysic we are testing. It is a simple technique for harboring, systematically, the thoughts and emotions we know are helpful. The technique is called 'treatment.' Traditional religions called it prayer, to be accompanied by prescribed physical postures. We prefer to avoid the word prayer because it carries the connotation of being a sort of begging letter or of expressing a wish for a far-off God to answer. Recently the media reported on a fond mother who prayed God to arrange for her veteran son to win the sweepstakes. In treatment we work not on God, but on ourselves. We become very still and center our thoughts on the Infinitude *in us* and all around us. By a series of mental exercises we ready ourselves to receive Its power and wisdom which is eternally available. We clear our minds of clutter, petty animosities, guilt, fear, peevishness and tension so that nothing will block the inflowing of All-knowingness. We identify with Life Itself and declare our willingness to "walk in Its ways."

Infinite Mind is often spoken of by the mystics as the "Ground of all being." In that limitless Ground each individual consciousness is a tiny acre. We must "dress it and

keep it" as the Voice told Adam to do. We prepare its sur-
face and sub-surface, keep it free of rock and thorn, keep
it fertile and tilled, ready to receive the energies forever
strewn throughout World Stuff. We must then choose
which seeds to plant, plant them carefully and continue to
tend them. Only thus can our acre of consciousness bear
fruit appropriate for us. "Keep thy heart with all dili-
gence," the ancient proverb warned. We must, with our
reasoning levels of mind, diligently befriend and tend the
subconscious levels, the heart in us. We must let no unconscious or pre-conscious drives clog the Power line.

For a good crop we must, like the farmer, in addition to
careful tending, let in light, warmth and rain from 'on
high.' We achieve our chosen goals only in proportion as
we keep our deep consciousness open to Infinitude. That
open-ness to the One Mind could, in former days, be
brought about in colorful church services resounding with
organ music and song. Large congregations intensified the
emotional impact. But in today's turmoil and skepticism
we need a more direct and personal experience of uplift
and belongingness. Also, rather than depend upon reiter-
ating well-worn supplications from the Book of Common
Prayer, we, in metaphysics, strive to give birth within our
private selves to a more immediate sense of Oneness.

We seek and find within ourselves the Deeper Mind and
know ourselves to be living, participating members of
Cosmic Being. We train and condition ourselves as deliberately as though we were preparing for a term exam or
the Superbowl. We set up a regimen of concentrated treatment sessions—like the coaching sessions of a tennis amateur with his pro—and then we spend the rest of our waking hours practicing what we have instructed ourselves to
do. Treatment and monitoring, these two steps are essential. Doing just the one or the other, and that with lapses,
is unlikely to get results. If we harbor contrary attitudes

between coaching sessions, we keep yanking the Law in opposing directions. Steady progress is made only if we get clear on our Oneness and then monitor, coax and persuade ourselves to follow through.

In athletics we can get trainers to keep us in trim, in metaphysical treatment we must do our own consistent self-disciplining. Or we can think of treatment in this way: to treat is to do for our own minds what the medical doctor does for our health problems. The physician calls on his schooling in biology and physiology, he calls on all his experience so that he will know the best way to explain the case. He then states his diagnosis and prescribes a remedy to counteract whatever he thinks caused the illness. He expects that his prescription will stimulate Mother Nature to do the actual healing. Before leaving he encourages his patient and assures him that recovery is ''on the way.''

Our work in treatment sessions falls easily, like the medical doctor's, into three steps. First we go to the Source of us; we connect with Omniscience, remind ourselves that It holds all wisdom and all energy. We invite, welcome and absorb all we can of It. Let us see this step as a tuning in, as making sure that our individual minds are open and receptive to wider knowledge and power. We call this first step 'alignment.'

Next we affirm our goals and describe the qualities and intensities of thought conducive to their manifesting. We must give attention to right attitudes, loving and symbiotic attitudes, and instruct ourselves to strengthen them. If we discover counterproductive thought patterns, it is important to prescribe a remedy which will stimulate new, correct attitudes. Though some metaphysicists use strong denials, stern and punishing, it seems more appropriate to reason gently with our subconscious and teach it better ways. This step we label 'affirmation.' As time goes on we often find additional mistaken attitudes which then call for changes in the treatment. Since Infinitude is a never-failing Supply and the Law a never-failing process, it matters not how often we re-word our affirmation. We must always remember that any shortfall in attaining our goals lies in our own inadequate attitudes and strategies.

The third step, 'acceptance,' is, of course, bolstering our own faith and confidence, our solid expectation that success is in process. We must be glad and grateful that what is in our minds matters, that we, the choosers, can let the Law work in us and for us, to manifest our good.

ALIGNMENT

The newcomer in metaphysics must pay special attention to this step in order to neutralize any lingering subconscious memories of an unbridgeable gap between man and the Most High. We must make sure we know that it is Mind that matters above and beyond all else. We delete any subliminal hindrances to the solid conviction that Mind is the Stuff of all that is, the Stuff that *we are*; Mind is not only "up there" and "out there," but *within* each one of us 'nearer to us than breathing.' Emerson put it this way—"God enters by a private door into every individual." (*Essay on Intellect*) In this prologos to our treatment we unlock that private door. We must become aware that whatever life, mentality, energy and stability we enjoy originates in That which for aeons has been called God. To grow and mature we must accept and reverence It. We must become aware that, without benefit of computer or machinery, by invisible in-being Mind designs and maintains Edelweiss and towering pine, bunny and butterfly, mouse and man.

Alignment must be not a short formal moment, like genuflecting in the church aisle, but rather a prolonged stay in hallowed closeness, a communion, a deeply felt belongingness. We must, as we do with music, get into the mood and spirit, respond to Its beauty, majesty and meaning.

We must come to know without shadow of doubt that we are centered in the one inexhaustible Givingness of life, intelligence and order. Our very desire opens us to a limitless inflow of Mind riches. Aligned with It, attuned to It, we rise above all confusion, fear, and weariness; we are newly inspired (breathed into), eager to be worthy of our Heritage. We put aside all problems of secular living, all attention to physical fitness and sensual excitement; we rest in "quietness and confidence"; we come to know the Self that is the self of us. However long it may take, we learn to be receptive, to entrust ourselves to the Oversoul, the One Source and Reality.

AFFIRMATION

Having established our alignment, our attunement, with the One Wholeness, we turn conscious attention to our own individual self and its interaction with the rest of the finite world. We state the current goal and outline as best we can the mental attitudes required. Though we cannot all be expert analysts, we can, as though in a series of confidential talks, acquaint ourselves with our true inwardness, reason with our subconscious and enlist its help. Centering upon one department of our lives per treatment, we describe the desired improvement and assert that we shall know how to make productive decisions, combine right ideas and take well-timed action. We make sure that the good desire harms no one and helps many. We try to discern what negative thought patterns we might have been harboring and declare them faded out, replaced by non-judging benevolence.

Though we are specific about our own attitudes and goals and joyously visualize how happy we shall be when they are attained, we do *not* specify just how they are to come about, what other persons are to do and when. This must be left entirely to the Law of Mind. Being neutral the Law maintains *universal* balance and responds to other persons' directions as well as to ours. The more intense our conviction (faith) that Infinite Mind works in us and through means of us, the sooner will our ideas condense into finite experience. When 'things go wrong' we fault not the 'things' but ourselves for possible non-love, doubt or fickleness. These flaws remind us that somewhere *in us,* we have harbored conflicting feelings or ideas.

This affirmation step is almost like making a list of jobs to do during the week; we cross off items and add others as the work goes on. We try to keep unmuddled; we mastermind ourselves into becoming, inwardly, the kind of persons who merit the goals we have set.

Age old notions about "miserable sinner," self-depreciation, must be gently—not forcibly—washed away. To say, "I'm stupid" or "Nobody loves me" is wishing just that upon ourselves. Nor do we slap down or quash aggressive stirrings which lurk in our psyche, we *educate* them into co-operating. Treatment is not scolding or 'psyching up'; it is self-therapy. Like competent psychologists who first of all establish rapport with the client, then patiently lead him to discover and heal himself, we must, in this step, respond to our inherited consciousness, make appropriate changes and decisions. We deliberately build a strong mental and emotional outlook and so become a more integrated, understanding and enterprising personality.

ACCEPTANCE

The third step in the concentrated coaching session is to accept, here and now, the good outcome of the treatment. No saying, "Well, we'll see," no "hoping"; we definitely state that our thinking has been intense enough to keep the Law consistently on the desired track. Even though the solution of the problem is not yet visible, we know and declare that in Mind Stuff it is already being accomplished. Time-lag occurs only on the finite, visible plane. We use the present tense—"I am being healed," "I am meeting congenial people," "I have the right job in the right place." To use the future tense would put the demonstration into the future.

In order to keep ourselves from mumbling parts of treatments *ad nauseam,* we close this step with a strong statement of acceptance, some phrase like "It is done" or "This is the truth and I act accordingly." Or we could just say "Period" or "Amen" as we return to the day's activities with goodwill and good cheer. Monitoring is now demanded, letting as few negative opinions as possible tinge the positive feelings we have prescribed for ourselves. In this day-long stream of mind meandering we can be our own "best pals" and with a kindly occasional push, keep ourselves on the track of "healthy-mindedness."

Knowing that we ourselves must do the work and do it so intelligently that when the Law manifests our goals, they will be as we planned, we must now buckle down to the composing and the doing of our treatments. Once the actual coaching session has begun, we want no fishing for the right words, no drifting off in mid-sentence. We must prepare the material and have it ready to present to our consciousness with full emphasis. We must tell ourselves in no uncertain terms.

fulfillment. There one can ask questions and become familiar with the terminology. Most of them have book tables and sell metaphysical magazines with ready-made treatments for every day in the month. These are of great value to newcomers. The printed words somehow have authority, especially when we realize that many thousands are reading the same words that same day, putting their faith in them. Joining the right group in metaphysics can do for the newcomer what joining a team does for an amateur athlete.

But groups are not available at the twice daily treatment times. Furthermore we must not become dependent on the thoughts of others. Each personality demands its own type of instruction. We all have predilections in language. Some published treatments are too Biblical for our taste, some too scientific; one phrase with the wrong connotations can spoil the impact of the entire treatment. True, we can take printed treatments and edit out what does not appeal, or combine parts of several treatments. Lacking a nearby metaphysical center and lacking even a magazine, we can begin by using the sample treatments given in my next chapter. But in the long run only we ourselves can express ideas in a way that deeply impresses us and fortifies our decisions. For each problem we face, a basic, custom-made treatment is a necessity—personally thought through, personally composed and personally declared.

The treatment should be written out. Why write? Because, no matter how we try, just thinking-along becomes vague and fleeting. Mere musing and pondering, no matter how pleasurable and edifying, lack the clarity we need in treating. Ruminating gets us nowhere. Even in mundane things like grocery shopping or weekend packing, we make lists. Using the correct words and making sentences will fasten down ideas which then form the basis for additional ideas. Thus we form a sort of scaffolding to which we can return in case we have wandered. While composing we may wander and retrace, but in the end we must have a coherent set of statements for self-instruction. In doing the treatment we must have no weak spots. No need to make a polished literary product—only to make it belong to us, convince us, *move us*.

Once composed and clearly printed out on a sturdy card this hand-made treatment will serve us for the beginning weeks. Twice daily, at times when we can be alone, we read it aloud. Why aloud? Because it is in our subconscious that at solemn points in our lives we *voice* declarations. Even today flag salutes, inaugurations and marriage vows are *voiced*. There are actual sensory reasons for this: in forming the words and then hearing them we double the sensory impact. Memorizing does not do as well because the words become automatic and we tend to rattle them off without thinking of the meaning. We must speak the treatment gently but firmly so that each time we do the treatment we erase a little more of the unwanted residue in the depths of us. There being no magnificent cathedral pageantry to impress and impassion us, we must do what we can with convincing ideas, sincere intention and avowed commitment.

Especially in the first step—Alignment—we must arrive at and maintain an altered state of consciousness. For that reason it is best to do only this step for the first several weeks. The purpose is fundamental: to establish our One-ness with the Infinite. For so many centuries we have been made to feel separate and unworthy. In metaphysics we must do the opposite, identify with It, align ourselves with It, do what Jesus meant when he said, "Seek ye first the Kingdom (the realm, the presence, the nearness) of God." We must make real to ourselves that It is within us, that we are in It, always have been, and always will be.

In composing the Alignment part of our treatment it is

good to use our favorite name for Infinitude and use it often. Because many moderns feel ambivalent about the name God, I have used it sparingly in this book. True, in my youth I argued that there could be no such thing as God, but while I was outgrowing my adolescent rejection of what seemed to me like a huge Dictator in the sky, I became very fond of many other names for the All-Giving-ness which *is* this cosmos. Use any name and as many names as appeal to you. We all have a good precedent for doing just that: in the Old Testament there were at least seven names. Yahweh, the name never to be pronounced, was revealed to Moses on the Mount and was declared to mean the "I AM," or "Ever-is-ness." The name Elohim emphasized the fullness and richness of the Almighty, and Shaddai was used in war situations. In writing this attune-ment section let us use the names we love best and in *doing* it, *voicing* it, let us savor their full significance.

In writing the second step, Affirmation, we state our in-tentions and describe the mental attitudes we feel would be helpful. As mentioned in the previous chapter, this step is likely to be modified as we reach some of our goals and envision others. When working for ourselves, we name the persons we wish to attract, or forgive, or be forgiven by. Mainly we instruct ourselves to be less stubborn, less angry, less frantic and more amiable, more free and coura-geous. Since we are simultaneously instructor and learner, we need to be clear and well organized. We must remem-ber that neither our reasoning mind nor our subconscious likes to be arrogantly ordered about. We do better with courteous 'requests.'

When treating for other persons, we speak their names so that the supremely intelligent Law may know whither to aim its workings. In metaphysical treatment we have the advantage that we need not, like the surgeon or psychia-trist, be in the immediate presence of the 'patient.' Divisions between physical and mental, here and there, spiritual and scientific, exist only on the finite level. On the Beyond level, everything is porous; intensified mental activity in one individual is revealed, as designated, in the other. The Law interflows all levels.

Practicing the Science of Mind or Religious Science principles does not demand that we use this type of treatment exclusively. Though treatment and monitoring should come first and be continuous, we do not scorn or condemn medical, surgical or psychiatric help. Such help, we have come to realize, also originates in Mind, also is other-regarding, and also operates under Mind Law. Combined, the two approaches hasten the cure. We must always know that the remedies and prognoses of clinical specialists can form a double attack on the faulty internal activity. Besides, laboratory tests can often give early warning of conditions which our mental work can then forestall. As we become convinced spiritually and therefore more effectual mentally, outside assistance will seldom be needed.

A caution: let not your enthusiasm bubble forth to family and friends. "See that thou tell no man," Jesus warned the leper whom he had helped. It is best to discuss our new philosophy and treatment work with no one. Outsiders delight in negative speculation and, like newsmen, run opinion polls on our diminishing chances. Their disbelief, even ridicule, also infects the Mind surrounding and indwelling you and becomes reverse treatment. We must persist in honest treatment and kindly monitoring in sweet privacy.

If, after what we think is sufficient treatment work our goals have not materialized, we must not give up. We must remember that the subconscious had deeply rooted mind patterns, cultural habits of unbelief and mistrust, which require far more self-discipline than smoke-ending or weightwatching. Though history tells of instantaneous cures and sudden insights—Meister Eckhart and Jacob Boehme, for instance—most of us are saturated with spiritual wretchedness. Our American philosopher-psychologist William James also described numerous sudden cures and mystical experiences resulting from New Thought teachings. But, in his Gifford Lectures (Edinburgh, 1901–1902), he devoted two chapters to overcoming the "misery habit," the "pining, puling, mumping mood" by "systematic healthy-mindedness." Metaphysical treatment for ourselves and for others must indeed be systematic and healthy-minded.

Seeming setbacks come to us because the Law encounters obstructive mind matters of which we are ignorant. Since we unwittingly send the Law on errands every waking and sleeping moment, not just in "yes" or "no" situations, we must be ever more thorough in treating and monitoring. We must, however, also realize that the process of growing up entails growing pains. A defeat or delay sometimes proves to be just the challenge that wakens new understanding, greater sensitivity and new inspiration. Some fine day while in the Prologos we shall discover what mistakes we have made and how to branch off in new directions of thought and action.

After the weeks of keeping aligned, keeping merged in Infinite Mind, and after additional weeks of composing and doing the Affirmations, improving them as we learn, we should have no trouble in making our statement of Acceptance. We simply assert that Omniscience and Its Law are at work in us and for us, manifesting right balance and right action. We assure ourselves that we can remain expectant of success because the intention, the quality and the intensity of our minds have set the direction for the infallible Law in finite mind, form and event. There is no need to treat again until the next scheduled session. We accept our good and rejoice. Amen, Amen.

Chapter Four

EXAMPLES OF TREATMENT

The sample treatments that follow will surely not be as effectual for the reader as they are for the writer, but they will be starting points. Since the Alignment step is so important in setting the inner tone, three examples are given. Unless and until we can do these wholeheartedly, without any reservations, until we feel comfortable with the metaphysical terms and meanings, the two following steps will be mere happy talk. This mental and emotional attunement with Infinite Mind is far more 'internal' than taking a medication. Alignment with the Most High could be compared with what we do with our radio and TV dials. On many different wavelengths, countless broadcasts are swirling about, day and night. What we hear and see depends on the set of our dial. So with Life Itself, with the Infinite, the Eternal, the Absolute, with Mind and Being. We are first of all receivers and then, under the Law of Mind, we are amateur senders. God sends unstintingly; it is we who must be willing to receive.

ALIGNMENT

PROLOGOS

The One Source is the source of me. Infinite Mind is the mind of me. The Allness which speeds the galaxies and burns in millions of stars, is the lifestream of me, flows through my veins and the deep of my mind. It is mine to accept, mine to build into my private being. It sets before me life and death, blessing and cursing. I choose life and blessing. Its riches and rightness are my guarantee that the fulfillment I seek, the decisions I make, are brought about. All the life, love, wisdom and joy I could desire abound in Infinitude. As I open my heart and mind, these blessings flow into my experience. With ears that really hear, I listen, appreciate and gratefully accept what is right for me. Though I am finite and unique, I am never separate; I am one with Eternal Mind, one with the cosmic Law, one with all nature and humanity. I, even I, am Infinitude revealing Itself in the world of form and event. I am a living, loving, self-accepting, self-perfecting partner in the Unbroken Wholeness. Amen.

ALIGNMENT

PROLOGOS

As a wavelet on the beach is born of the mighty ocean, as the snowflake belongs to the blizzard, so do I belong to the One Life. As the air I breathe interflows me and all that I see and touch, so does Infinite Mind interflow my finite world. Made of the same Mind Stuff, I belong to all things great and small, to the wondrousness of stars and moons, to the miracles of conception, birth, life and death. I open myself to Totality, to Its myriad energies, pulsing, intertwining, dissolving and re-combining, to the Uncreate becoming creation. I let Its Omniscience pour into me, drench me with the wisdom I personally need. Enlightened, enriched and fortified, I begin to understand the world, to feel connectedness, love, side-by-sideness, veneration. I am linked and united with all creation, with all-in-the-One and the One-in-all. Day by day, in my private world, I know what I need to know, what I need to do and how I must do it. Right feeling and right thinking are born in me so that the Law can produce right results in, and through means of me. I am Omnipotence in action—now. This is the truth of me forever.

ALIGNMENT

PROLOGOS

In the beginning God, the Voice, the Word, the Primal Mind, the Be-ingness of all that ever was or will be. Here and now I realize that there is no emptiness, that the stuff of the world is Mind Stuff, fluidic, dynamic, forever becoming form, dissolving and becoming new form. It is infinite, alive, intelligent, co-ordinated. How else could man make sense of It, harness and rely on Its energies? I now realize that no tiniest organism is separate from the Lifestream of the cosmos, that all is alive with Life Itself. How then can I be separate? As Infinitude cradles the galaxies, as the Milky Way cradles our sun and its planets, as my bloodstream nourishes the organs and cells of my body, so does Total Mind cradle and nourish my private mind. At last I understand that there can be no ceiling between me and the Most High. I now cease rejecting Its riches and rightness. I invite It to reveal the secrets of Its Way and Truth. Putting away all confusion and unbelief, I listen and perceive new meanings, new ideas, new power. I am at one with Life Itself, with my world and my innermost self. All is well, Amen, Amen.

COMPLETE TREATMENTS

MY WORLD IS A FRIENDLY WORLD

Alignment

Here and now I stop thinking of myself as a frightened soul in a crowd of angry people. I take time to breathe deeply of the Onliness which indwells this entire cosmos. As an incarnation of that Onliness I am not weak and vulnerable. There is no cause for me to be a frightened soul. I do not need to hide behind a mask of arrogance. The power and wisdom of the One Mind become my private mind, more than adequate for every occasion. I drop the silly mask and admit that what I have been seeing is just what, in my anguish of separateness, I expected to see. I realize that my world has been mirroring back my own stern attitude and bold image.

Affirmation

I now let the true Self of me shine through. I am able and unafraid. I look, not for hostility, but for peace and kindliness. As I erase fear, the Law of Mind produces for me ample understanding, respect and co-operation. My new courage and confidence change my image and the world mirrors back my new-found goodwill and friendliness. I consistently expect harmony and collaboration and I consistently find just that.

Acceptance

By the action of the One Law I meet new minds, free, creative minds. In our togetherness we share ideas, bring forth new relationships and constructive events. We enrich the world with new insight into Truth. Under the Law of Mind it is already being done. I rejoice and act accordingly. Amen.

JANE AND JERRY ENJOY PROSPERITY

Alignment

Inexhaustible is the richness of Infinitude. However great and varied the powers of science, vastly greater are the resources of Eternal Mind. Jane and Jerry are in harmony and alignment with that Mind. They know that Its limitless abundance awaits their individual acceptance. Therefore from out of Totality they select and utilize what combinations of ideas and powers are appropriate to their finite needs.

Affirmation

Jane and Jerry keep in accord with the All-Givingness. They harbor vivid and dynamic thoughts of success and plenty. They know that prosperity is theirs to earn. They know that Mind is the only investment from which profit can be gained. They rejoice in a rich inflow of intelligent ideas. As opportunities develop, they are recognized and acted upon. Ample income results. In easy co-operation and without depriving anyone, Jane and Jerry build a comfortable, prosperous outer life to express their unfailing Oneness with the Infinite. They have and appreciate peace, wealth and benevolence.

Acceptance

Wealth of spirit, mind and material things appear in their lives. They delight not only in ample money but in the

wondrousness of the One Life. Ever mindful of the Source
they receive gratefully and spend wisely. They keep attuned and the Law produces. Amen, Amen, Amen.

I AM IN EXCELLENT HEALTH

Alignment
The One Unbroken Wholeness is mine at all times. It is the
Source and Substance of my being. I welcome Its inpour-
ing vitality, I let It refresh, renew and replenish every part
and process of my mind and body. Its fullness restores all
energies I have allowed to diminish. I am now receptive to
the dynamic inflow of mental and physical Perfection.

Affirmation
This very minute I remind myself that I am well, strong
and effectual in any action I decide to take. All thought of
weakness or disability vanishes. I know that I can easily do
my usual work and I proceed to do just that. I am as
vigorous as I want to be and I keep wanting to be as sturdy
and vigorous as I ever was. I erase whatever fleeting ideas
of weakness I may have been tolerating. I know that I am
a perfect physical organism functioning perfectly. I have
ample vitality and endurance. Without strain or undue
fatigue I accomplish what I plan to do. I respond con-
fidently to the demands of my days for I know that the
unlimited Wholeness of Life Itself is mine.

Acceptance
Because I accept the unfailing energies of Life Itself, I am
in exuberant health. I use my strength intelligently,
balancing work and rest. I balance mental and physical action, maintaining confidence in the One Great Law. I am
fit because I know I am Life personified. This is the truth
and I act accordingly. Period.

I FIND FULFILLMENT

Alignment

Life Itself, Infinite Mind, lives in me as the uniqueness which I have chosen to be. Infinite Mind is the garden in which I grow. Increasingly I sense and absorb Its harmony and completeness. Constantly I perceive more, and respond better, to all the aspects of Its unfailing abundance.

Affirmation

Young as I am, flexible, growing, eager to achieve, determined to assert my worth, I become aware that my growing must not be haphazard. Systematically I melt away doubt and confusions. I allow no insecurity-thoughts to linger in my subconscious. Consciously I welcome the specific qualities of Mind which can enhance my uniqueness. I re-survey the mind patterns of my past; when I find contrary tendencies I learn to counteract them. I keep account of any weakness and gradually transform it into strength. As I better understand myself I find greater appreciation for the others in my world. Observing that my attitudes influence their attitudes, that situations mellow when there is gentleness, I move gently among them, respecting their uniqueness and expressing mine. I discover new potentials within me and move into my rightful place in the world around me.

Acceptance

My inner life is rich and joyous. In the outer world I am humane, mature, a valued person. In all my ways I find fulfillment. This is the joy of knowing that I am in-and-of the One Mind and Its Law. Increasingly, I find fulfillment. Amen.

Chapter Five

AFTERWORD

If we persevere in thus building and monitoring our consciousness, some fine morning we shall realize that our metaphysical credo is no longer merely a logical hypothesis. We shall no longer need to think it out, reason ourselves into it—we identify with it. We come to know that it is not just a creed but the truth by which we live. We are constantly aware of the Beyond in the near. This inner sense of belonging underlies all the activities of our outer world. True, we tend and cherish our inwardness, we treat, we attend meetings and seminars, we rejoice to find in age-old and brand new writings, instances of the principles once so strange to us. But we do not desert the temporal, secular, everyday world.

Unlike many religious enthusiasts who become hermits to sanctify themselves with poverty and endless prayer, the metaphysicist holds to the premise that the finite world, flawed and perishable though it may be, is none other than a miniscule embodiment of Life Imperishable. Our way is not detachment but an ever more sensitive attachment, a relatedness, a side-by-side-ness with all creations of the Uncreate. We venerate both the "Kingdom" and that which is 'of the earth, earthy.'

Two superb examples of merging the inner with the outer world are the lives of Gautama Buddha and Jesus of

Nazareth. The Hindu prince, having by accident seen
something of human misery, spurned the worldly customs
of the palace and sought truth among the hermit sages. He
detached himself from the outer world with such radical
asceticism that he collapsed from undernourishment.
When, helped by country folk, he recovered consciousness
he knew first-hand that living in the inner world *only* was
not the Way of serenity. The next forty years he spent centering on the everyday world, teaching the Eightfold Path
to right living and right trading with one's fellow man.

Just as the Buddha modified the ancient Hindu tradition so did Jesus, five hundred years later, reinterpret his
inherited doctrine. With far more emphasis on the
Indwelling Spirit than one finds in Buddhism, the Carpenter's Son taught the multitudes to be ever-mindful of
the Infinite while living in the finite. His Beatitudes deal
with human happiness through matching one's actions
among men with the Allgivingness of the Father Indwelling. His was the equation: "Be ye therefore perfect, even
as your Father which is in heaven (Infinitude) is perfect."

Through the centuries since these teachings, man of the
West has allowed the outer world, the now mechanized
world, to dominate. He has for the most part clung to that
material world and destroyed the balance between his
spiritual and his intellectual evolution. He has allowed the
physical, sensual, definable desires to outweigh the deep
yearnings of the self which, in reality, he is. High time now
for him to accept the next modification of his Story, a new
frame of reference, the new meta-physic. The seesawing of
human development must abate. A steadier, coordinated
pace is required to thread a trail through polluted environment, dehumanized society and the nuclear perils that intellect has spawned.

The metaphysical credo reveals that being finite—having limits—is not a sin but rather an opportunity to choose

Centers for Metaphysical Studies

Divine Science Federation International
   1819 East Fourteenth Street
   Denver, Colorado 80218

International New Thought Alliance
   7314 East Stetson Drive
Scottsdale, Arizona 85251

Religious Science International
   3130 Fifth Avenue
   San Diego, California 92103

United Church of Religious Science
   3251 West Sixth Street
   P. O. Box 75127
   Los Angeles, California 90075

Unity School of Christianity
   Unity Village, Missouri 64065

By writing to any of these headquarters
a list of their member churches
and copies of their magazines
can be obtained

READING LIST

JACK ENSIGN ADDINGTON. *Psychogenesis*. New York: Dodd, Mead and Company, 1971.

Adventures of the Mind. Collection from Saturday Evening Post. New York: Alfred Knopf, Borzoi Books, 1960.

DONALD HATCH ANDREWS. *The Symphony of Life*. Lee's Summit, Mo.: Unity Books, 1966.

RICHARD BACH. *Jonathan Livingston Seagull*. New York: Macmillan Company, 1970.

FREDERICK W. BAILES. *Your Mind Can Heal You*. New York: Dodd, Mead and Company, 1941.

Hidden Power for Human Problems. Englewood Cliffs, N.J.: Prentice-Hall, Inc., 1957.

RAYMOND CHARLES BARKER. *Treat Yourself to Life*. New York: Dodd, Mead and Company, 1954.

The Power of Decision. New York: Dodd, Mead and Company, 1968.

The Science of Successful Living. New York: Dodd, Mead and Company, 1957.

LINCOLN BARNETT. *The Universe and Dr. Einstein*. New York: William Sloane Associates, 1957.

N. J. BERRILL. *You and the Universe*. New York: Fawcett World Library Premier Book, 1963.

Man's Emerging Mind. New York: Fawcett World Library Premier Book, 1962.

Bhagavad-Gita. Translated by Prabhavananda and Christopher Isherwood. New York: New American Library of World Literature, Inc., 1954.

The Holy Bible. King James version. Any edition.

RICHARD MAURICE BUCKE, M. D. *Cosmic Consciousness*. New York: E. P. Dutton and Company, Inc., 1954.

The Teachings of the Compassionate Buddha. New York: New American Library of World Literature, Inc., Mentor Book, 1963.

H. EMILIE CADY. *Lessons in Truth*. Unity Village, MO: Unity Books, 1895.

JOSEPH CAMPBELL. *Hero with a Thousand Faces*. Cleveland, OH: World Publishing Company, Meridian Books, 1974.

The Masks of God—Primitive Mythology. New York: The Viking Press, 1974.

FRITJOF CAPRA. *The Tao of Physics*. Boulder, CO: Shambhala, 1975.

PIERRE TEILHARD DE CHARDIN. *The Phenomenon of Man*. New York: Harper and Brothers, 1959.

Building the Earth. Wilkes Barre, PA: Dimension Books, 1965.

Any others.

HENRY DRUMMOND. *Natural Law in the Spiritual World*. New York: James Pott and Company, 1885.

WILL DURANT. *The Story of Philosophy*. New York: Simon and Schuster, 1927.

RALPH WALDO EMERSON. *Selected Essays*. New York: Washington Square Press, 1965.

WARREN P. EVANS. *Mental Cure*. Boston: Colby and Rich, 1885.

Primitive Mind Cure. Boston: H. H. Carter and Karrick, 1886.

FRANK G. GOBLE. *The Third Force*. New York: Grossman Publishers, 1970.

EDGAR J. GOODSPEED. *The Story of the Bible*. Chicago:
University of Chicago Press, 1936.

MANLY PALMER HALL. *Twelve World Teachers*. Los Angeles, CA: The Philospher's Press, 1937.

Old Testament Wisdom. Los Angeles, CA: Philosophical
Research Society, Inc., 1957.

Any others.

PRESTON HAROLD. *The Shining Stranger*. New York:
Dodd, Mead and Company, Wayfarer Press. Copyright
Gerald Heard, 1967.

GERALD HEARD. *Is God Evident?* London: Faber and
Faber, Ltd., 1950.

The Human Venture. New York: Harper and Brothers,
1955.

Training for a Life of Growth. Santa Monica, CA:
Wayfarer Press, 1960.

ERNEST HOLMES. *The Science of Mind*. New York: Dodd,
Mead and Company, 1950.

It's Up to You. Los Angeles, CA: Scrivener and Company,
1948.

Creative Mind and Success. New York: Dodd, Mead and
Company, 1962.

Any and all others.

FRED HOYLE. *The Nature of the Universe*. New York:
Harper and Brothers, 1950.

Frontiers of Astronomy. New York: New American
Library, Mentor Book, 1957.

ALDOUS HUXLEY. *The Perennial Philosophy*. New York:
Harper and Brothers, 1954.

JULIAN HUXLEY. *Religion Without Revelation*. New York:
Harper and Brothers, 1957.

WILLIAM JAMES. *Varieties of Religious Experience*. New York: Random House, Modern Library, 1902.

RAYNOR C. JOHNSON. *The Imprisoned Splendour*. New York: Harper and Row, 1953.

A Religious Outlook for Modern Man. London: Hodder and Stoughton, 1963.

CARL GUSTAV JUNG. *The Undiscovered Self*. New York: Little, Brown and Company, Inc., Mentor Book, 1959.

LAOTZU. *The Way of Life*. American Version by Witter Bynner. New York: The John Day Company, 1944.

Letters of a Scattered Brotherhood. Edited by Mary Strong. New York: Harper and Brothers, 1948.

PIERRE LECOMTE DU NOÜY. *Human Destiny*. New York: Longmans Green and Company, 1947.

JOSHUA LOTH LIEBMAN. *Peace of Mind*. New York: Simon and Schuster, 1946.

LAWRENCE LE SHAN. *The Medium, the Mystic and the Physicist*. New York: The Viking Press, 1974.

ROLLO MAY. *Man's Search for Himself*. New York: Dell Publishing Company by arrangement with W. W. Norton, 1953.

Love and Will. New York: Dell Publishing Company by arrangement with W.W. Norton, 1969.

ELAINE PAGELS. *The Gnostic Gospels*. New York: Random House, Inc., 1979.

Philosophers of Science. New York: Carlton House. Copyright by Random House, Inc., 1947.

JOHN R. PLATT. *Perception and Change, Projections for Survival*. Ann Arbor, MI: University of Michigan Press. 1970.

IRA PROGOFF. *Jung's Psychology and Its Social Meaning*. New York: Julian Press, 1953.

The Symbolic and the Real. New York: Julian Press, Inc., 1963.

The Death and Rebirth of Psychology. New York: Julian Press, Inc., 1969.

The Cloud of Unknowing. New York: Julian Press, Inc., 1957.

Jung's Synchronicity and Human Destiny. New York: Dell Publishing Company by arrangement with Julian Press, 1973.

The White Robed Monk. New York: Dialogue House Library, 1977.

The Well and the Cathedral. New York: Dialogue House Library, 1977.

The Quimby Manuscripts. Horatio W. Dresser, Editor. New York: The Julian Press, 1961.

ERVIN SEALE. *The Great Prayer.* New York: The Builder Press, 1947.

Take Off From Within. New York: Harper and Row, 1971.

Any and all Builder Press pamphlets.

HARLOW SHAPLEY. *Beyond the Laboratory.* New York: Charles Scribner's Sons, 1967.

EDMUND W. SINNOTT. *The Biology of the Spirit.* New York: The Viking Press, 1955.

Cell and Psyche. New York: Harper and Brothers, Torch Books, 1961.

CUSHING SMITH. *I Can Heal Myself and I Will.* New York: Frederick Fell, 1962.

JAN CHRISTIAN SMUTS. *Holism and Evolution.* New York: The Viking Press, Compass Books, 1961.

ALVIN TOFFLER. *Future Shock.* New York: Random House, 1970.

THOMAS TROWARD. *The Dore Lectures.* 1909. New York: Robert H. McBride and Company. 12th printing, 1940.

The Edinburgh Lecures on Mental Science. 1909. New York: Dodd, Mead and Company. 27th printing.

Bible Mystery and Bible Meaning. 1913. New York: Dodd, Mead and Company. 21st printing.

The Creative Process in the Individual. New York: Dodd, Mead and Company. 22nd printing, 1962.

The Law and the Word. New York: Dodd, Mead and Company. 17th printing, 1953.

EVELYN UNDERHILL. *Practical Mysticism.* New York: E. P. Dutton and Company, Inc., 1960.

Mysticism. New York: E. P. Dutton and Company, Inc., 1961.

CARL HERMANN VOSS. *The Universal God.* Boston: Beacon Paperback, 1961.

LYALL WATSON. *Supernature.* New York: Doubleday and Company, 1973.

H. G. WELLS. *The Outline of History.* New York: The Macmillan Company, 1921.

ALFRED NORTH WHITEHEAD. *Adventures of Ideas.* New York: Mentor Book by arrangement with the Macmillan Company, 1955.

JOHN K. WILLIAMS. *The Wisdom of Your Subconscious Mind.* Englewood Cliffs, N. J.: Prentice-Hall, Inc., 1964.